Claim Your Dream Life

"If you're anything like me, you absolutely want to *Claim Your Dream Life*. What does that even mean? Are you intrigued? If so, this is a must read and a plan you will want to carefully consider--a detailed, clear and a complete roadmap to paradise--your paradise, whatever that means to you. Enjoy!"

Jill Lublin, 4x Best-Selling Author,
International Speaker, Master Publicity Strategist

"I love the book as a blueprint for possibilities--who doesn't want to move to paradise and spend their days in the sun and sand? I love the person behind the book even more because she walks the walk and now wants to share the talk with others. Dawn paints a beautiful picture of what can happen when you take command, make a decision, plan carefully and execute - and gives you the full step-by-step process without holding back. She shares her expertise as well as the dream she and her husband made come true--so you can do the same and define your own dream life. Brilliant!"

Ridgely Goldsborough, Best Selling Author of
The Great Ones and International Speaker

"If you've ever fantasized about living in a distant paradise, an international hub, or any beautiful location overseas, here is your unequivocal invitation to chase those dreams. Dawn Fleming's thorough, fully researched and fully explained advice is accumulated over decades of personal experience. An experienced traveler, entrepreneur, international business attorney, and lifestyle consultant, Dawn's central message is: "No matter where you are in life, everyone has dreams to discover and pursue.""

Marika Flatt, Travel Editor, Texas Lifestyle Magazine

"Dawn is a master Communicator. She's done a wonderful job of organizing content and delivering it in a logical easy-to-understand manner. She has demystified the entire process of moving overseas."

Diane Huth, Best Selling Author of
Brand You! To Land Your Dream Job

"*Claim Your Dream Life* came at the right time and most importantly, with the right information! I was thrilled to discover that although I don›t know exactly what I want, *Claim Your Dream Life* has given me the jump start I need to figure it out. Filled with real-world examples, thoughtful, self-discovery-driving questions, and very specific "how to's", this book leaves you feeling inspired and motivated to take the actions needed to create your roadmap to start making it happen. Thank you, Dawn!"

Terri Zelasko, Dallas, Texas

"I loved the easy reading of *Claim Your Dream Life*. I greatly appreciated Dawn's frank and eye opening discussion of what ails the United States, without getting on a political soapbox. Her exercises have been thought through and perhaps most importantly, have stimulated and guided conversations with my wife. It has definitely helped us in making positive life choices."

Mick Niess, Sioux Falls, South Dakota

"Paradise, maybe...shoestring...not necessarily. I mean this book isn't for those dreaming of 'pie in the sky', unless it's pizza in Italy! Nor is it for those in their 20's trekking aimlessly around Europe flinging their backpacks. Dawn's book has sound actionable ideas for midlife adults. Real experiences, from real people you can learn from to make it happen in the best way for you. A must read, and a great gift idea."

George White, International House Sitter in Rome, Italy

"Don't reinvent the wheel. Someone already did the tough part to make our life easier. Dawn and Tom have made the journey. This is the map with guidelines for you to claim your dream life. Avoid some of the common potholes and issues that happen to everyone. Make your journey easier and far more fun."

Darren Howarter, American Expat in Medellin, Colombia

"The book is fun, simple (a compliment), practical fun tools that are easy to understand and implement and realistic with real life examples and stories. It covers all the good and challenging aspects that one may experience along the way including all the main topics that need to be addressed. It shows many ways of starting the process and achieving the goal, highlighting the need for a plan with milestones. I like Dawn's call to think through the whole process."

Helene Raison, French Expat in Dallas, Texas

"More than an interesting idea, this book makes the possibility of retiring in a tropical location a tempting prospect. Fleming fleshes out a systematic plan to help the reader know themselves and their goals first, and then outlines the way to achieve them."

Tess Scott, Sarnia, Ontario, Canada

CLAIM YOUR DREAM LIFE

How to Retire in Paradise
on a Shoestring Budget

DAWN FLEMING

NEW YORK

LONDON • NASHVILLE • MELBOURNE • VANCOUVER

Claim Your Dream Life

How to Retire in Paradise on a Shoestring Budget

Published in New York, New York, by Morgan James Publishing. Morgan James is a trademark of Morgan James, LLC. www.MorganJamesPublishing.com

Proudly distributed by Ingram Publisher Services.

Morgan James BOGO™

A **FREE** ebook edition is available for you or a friend with the purchase of this print book.

CLEARLY SIGN YOUR NAME ABOVE

Instructions to claim your free ebook edition:
1. Visit MorganJamesBOGO.com
2. Sign your name CLEARLY in the space above
3. Complete the form and submit a photo of this entire page
4. You or your friend can download the ebook to your preferred device

ISBN 9781631956652 paperback
ISBN 9781631956669 ebook
Library of Congress Control Number: 2021939918

Cover Design by:
Megan Dillon
megan@creativeninjadesigns.com

Interior Design by:
Chris Treccani
www.3dogcreative.net

Morgan James is a proud partner of Habitat for Humanity Peninsula and Greater Williamsburg. Partners in building since 2006.

Get involved today! Visit MorganJamesPublishing.com/giving-back

TABLE OF CONTENTS

ACKNOWLEDGMENTS

I wanted to start by thanking my incredible husband Tom Clifford for being an unwavering collaboration partner for over 20 years during the journey to create our Dream Life. Without his love, support, and faith in what was possible this book would never have been written. When we met we were two individuals who had been knocked down repeatedly but survived somehow and became friends. I never expected to remarry and I'm filled with gratitude each and every day to be blessed with a life partner who truly believes in me. His patience, kindness and wisdom allow me to be who I am at my core without reservation.

I want to thank my dear friend Diane Huth for her inspiration to finally write this book after dreaming about it for more than a decade. Her enthusiasm and marketing expertise were an invaluable contribution. I want to thank Steve Burgess for helping me discover my freedom formula, Jane Deuber for her support in finding my voice, Gail Minogue for sharing her expertise about cycles, seasons and being in flow with universal energy, Melissa Ricker for showing me how to provide value not only to my clients but also how to pour into and serve a larger community who don't become clients, Sundae Bean for the inspiration and courage to launch my podcast and her undying dedication to serving the globally mobile community.

I'm so grateful for my Dream Life Academy members ("Dream Lifers") they have eagerly absorbed my teachings and applied them to achieve lightening speed results. Because of their success I have become addicted to helping make even more dreams come true. Thank you to Dream Lifer Susan Santilena and Glenda Garman for their editing expertise and support. I also want thank the Claim Your Dream Life Facebook Community for their support as I tested to see what worked and made adjustments based on their feedback. This book is infinitely better because of your real-world application of these concepts.

I also know that none of this would be possible if it weren't for my Overseas Life Redesign Podcast guests and listeners. The guests eagerly and kindly supplied the stories of their successes and mistakes. Each story offers so much value to those interested in taking the same path. There are so many amazing people who are part of my journey, it would be impossible to name them all.

Thank you.

By Sundae Schneider-Bean

"Paradise" and "shoestring budget" don't seem to go together quite like other more famous pairings, such as peanut butter and jelly, surf and turf or even the birds and the bees. Dawn Fleming, in *Claim Your Dream Life: How to Retire in Paradise on a Shoestring Budget*, invites you to experience your life as paradise and says you can do so on an affordable budget. Sound ambitious? Good, then you are in the right place.

Helping people transform ambitious desires into real-life results is deep in my bones. As an intercultural strategist, a life transition facilitator and solution-oriented coach, I have helped individuals from over 60 countries across six continents navigate through (and flourish beyond!) major life and geographical transitions. One of the most meaningful aspects of my work is watching individuals achieve their deepest desires, and part of how they get there is through a vision, proven strategies and the right mindset. That is what this book is about to offer you.

I have had the pleasure of knowing Dawn Fleming since she became part of my community and program Expat Coach

Coalition - a select group of practitioners and coaches serving expats. It was immediately clear that she, too, was deeply committed to getting proven strategies in the hands of more people so they can make the most of their lives abroad.

This book is Dawn's battle cry, her answer to the call when midlife beckons you for a reset. Claim Your Dream Life is about possibilities. It is simultaneously an invitation and a road map for how to break through limiting beliefs, dare to dream and take courageous yet practical action that will lead you to your ideal life.

Dawn's unique perspective and 30 years of experience shine through in this book as a delightful combination of one-part dreamer, one-part sensible attorney and one-part savvy business owner. Each element is stronger and richer due to the presence of the other.

Dawn's enthusiasm and commitment to supporting you as you walk the road she, too, has traveled is tangible. As she shares real-life stories and alerts you to potential challenges ahead, she makes transparent what it really takes to transform your dreams into reality. Every step of the way, she also helps you see that it's possible.

One of the driving principles in my work is to live without regret. Do not let one of them be an unanswered call for a midlife reset. If you have a dream in your heart to live abroad, this book gives you an inspiring yet practical blueprint for how you can do that. Thanks to Dawn's insight and expertise, she helps you see how "paradise" paired with "budget" can be delicious.

Sundae Schneider-Bean is Creator of Adapt & Succeed Abroad, Founder of Expat Coach Coalition, Podcast host of Expat Happy Hour, Leader of Expats on Purpose

CHAPTER 1

Claiming Your Dream Life

Did you ever go on a vacation and never want to go home? Have you been thinking about living overseas for years? Do you believe it is even possible? Are you living your dream life?

In these pages, I hope to inspire the courageous action that turns dreams into reality. To help you understand that it is okay for you to be happy. To encourage you to not settle for what is realistic, practical, or expected. To not live a life based on "should" or the expectations of others. To remove the limits we impose on ourselves and not let your dreams remain dreams. Life has an expiration date. Don't wait until it is too late.

Over the last century we have seen profound shifts. In the United States, average life expectancy in 1900 was 48 years, in 2050 it is predicted to jump to 85 years. In 1900 there were 3 million people aged 65 or older, in 2000 there were 35 million.

Models predict there will be 86 million people over age 65 by 2050. Over the last 100 years we have been gifted an entire adult lifetime.

This change presents us with both challenges and opportunities. Many people are falling behind financially or fearful of outliving their retirement funds while the cost of living continues to go up. Companies continue to add more and more contract workers instead of full-time employees to keep overhead costs low and flexibility high. Pensions have become obsolete and generous benefit packages rare.

Students of all ages are taking on staggering debt loads, earning diplomas but not learning the high demand skills the marketplace requires. The rules have changed, the economy has changed. Change is to be expected but today it is happening at an incredibly accelerated pace. There is no roadmap to navigate and thrive amid all these changes. This book shares the stories of people who have adapted to these societal changes and how they did it!

I had an amazing career as an international business attorney, but it did not make me happy. When I realized that practicing law would not give me the lifestyle I wanted, I found a way out. I wanted to have a great quality of life and, to me, that meant being happy, healthy, and a valuable member of a loving community.

Today I'm a non-practicing attorney and serial entrepreneur with over 30 years of experience in setting up, marketing, managing and maintaining thriving businesses. After retiring as an attorney, I became a top producer and popular sales trainer in the relationship marketing industry. For two decades I mentored and coached people to become more than they ever thought possible. It was a great experience. But I always knew I was destined for more.

I have completely started over, changed my life, changed my career, created new lifestyles, and moved to places where I literally knew no one, not once or twice or three times but four moves to completely new locations. I have been fortunate to have incredible experiences. I am blessed to have met wonderful people and made lifelong friends along the way.

In this book, I share the process that empowered me to blaze a trail, take risks, make uncomfortable changes, and audaciously go after the lifestyle of my dreams. We live in a globally mobile economy that presents many new opportunities that never existed before and I took full advantage of them.

When my husband Tom and I lived in Southern California, we had successful businesses until 2008, when we didn't. Our lives were a blur, hustle and grind, wash, rinse, repeat day after day. We were living a fast-paced schedule with never enough time. We were making great incomes, but money flowed out just as fast as it came in. Maybe you can relate? When it became clear that we could no longer hold onto our past careers, businesses, and real estate investments, we simply let go.

We had waited until our comfort zone was so uncomfortable, we had to make a change. You have probably heard the phrase "jump and the net will appear". We did just that! Was it scary? Yes! It would have been so much easier had we known what was waiting for us.

In 2010, we left Southern California and sailed 5,000 miles through the Panama Canal to Florida, where we lived for six years. Moving to Florida was good for us but it still did not feel like home. We yearned for a vibrant community, a beach lifestyle, and richer cultural experiences. We packed the sailboat and began a voyage of discovery that led us back to Isla Mujeres, a tropical island in the Caribbean. The place fit. We stayed and are living our dream.

In Chapter 2, you will find a fun exercise. If you take it seriously, it can shift your thought process and open up an entire world of possibilities for your future.

Today we own and run a stunning oceanfront vacation villa, Castillito del Caribe, and Integrity Vacation Property Management. We own and operate Overseas Life Redesign, a coaching and consulting business teaching others to discover their dreams and turn them into reality just as we did.

A common theme I hear from my Overseas Life Redesign podcast guests is the sense of community they gain because of their overseas move. They joined like-minded people (expats) who left their home country, and now feel at home in a new country. They appreciate being part of a culture that values community, the wisdom of elders and caring for each other.

Our associations matter, so we must choose them wisely. We need to be around people who allow us to feel safe, to be our true selves, to feel loved and supported without judgment or criticism. With modern technology, people are more connected now than any time in history, but in many ways, are so alone. Our souls yearn to belong, to be connected to something bigger and to each other.

When I think back about the most difficult period of my life, the divorce from my first husband, I distinctly remember a major turning point. A friend suggested I check out a nonreligious divorce recovery program offered by a local church. I will never forget the feeling I had just walking through the door. The sanctuary was packed with about 500 people. They were all going through a divorce just like me. I felt like the weight of the world was lifted and things got so much better for me just by being in a community. I no longer felt so alone.

According to Robert D Putnam in *Bowling Alone: The Collapse and Revival of American Community,* "As a rule of thumb, if you belong to no groups but decide to join one, you cut your risk of dying over the next year by 50%. If you smoke and belong to no groups, it's a toss-up statistically whether you should stop smoking or start joining."

A further survey conducted by the health provider Cigna, revealed widespread loneliness with nearly half of all Americans reporting they feel alone, isolated or left out at least a part of the time. In addition, the survey showed 54% of respondents feel that no one knows them well, and 40% report lack of companionship, and say relationships are not meaningful, and they are isolated from others. These are not good numbers, especially when looking at the direct impact these findings have on physical health and quite frankly, the health of society. The bottom line is we all need loving, healthy relationships and communities of belonging for optimal health.

Using our experience, the experiences of others and the latest research, we developed a vision for our business. To grow an Overseas Life Redesign community to encourage connections, build communities that foster compassion, create environments for embracing individual uniqueness and encourage others to do the same.

If you, dear reader, have few or no dreams or have lost hope, this book is for you. You can learn to dream again. The future is filled with inspired possibilities. If you have dreamed of adventure, if you are not sure what life holds in middle life or after, I promise that your mind will be racing with excitement by the time you are finished reading. Your current circumstances do not have to dictate your future.

Early in our relationship I asked my husband Tom to attend a personal development workshop. The trainer asked everyone to write down a list of their dreams. The exercise made Tom extremely uncomfortable because at age 50, he had no dreams. He now admits that at the time he was a walking cadaver. He was twice divorced, he had lost his aerospace engineering business in bankruptcy and survived melanoma, all while raising his two boys as a single parent. It took him a while to begin to dream again, to imagine what the future might hold. His advice "Keep at it. It gets easier with practice".

Today I see myself as an alchemist, an expert at change. I have a burning desire to help others through life's transitions. My goal is to provide inspiration along with a roadmap that worked for us and many others, plus practical tools, step-by-step methods, and a supportive community of like-minded people.

In this book, I use personal stories to illustrate life-changing results from the live workshops, attended by hundreds seeking their dreams. Many workshop attendees have gone through them multiple times because they are so impactful.

Paul attended my workshop twice. After the first workshop ended, he sent me a heartwarming but gut wrenching email about the past thirteen years of his life. He was broken, having experienced divorce, financial devastation, a resurgence of PTSD and later addiction to pain meds, the death of a son and more! He said he was in what he called the winter of his life, beaten down with no dreams or hope for the future. Paul told me that learning the content and doing the action steps, had a profound impact on him. It had taken him out of winter into spring and summer. He had a newfound hope and a clear vision of what was possible!

To continue his journey of reinvention, Paul joined my Dream Life Academy. He flew down to Isla Mujeres, Mexico for a one-month "Beta Test" to see if he would like to live here. He did, very much. Paul returned to Canada spent time with his family for the holidays and returned to Isla to live full time. He had met Diane, another "Dream Lifer" (Academy member) during his beta test and they had hit it off at once. When Paul returned from Canada, he brought an engagement ring. Diane said yes. Who knows, if you are seeking a life companion, perhaps you will find them in this tribe.

While there are lots of books to help with the mechanics of moving overseas, the financial benefits and logistics of retiring overseas, this book is for people who want to dream again, to explore new possibilities in middle life, for those who feel a deep void and know something important is missing.

This book will help you to *Claim Your Dream Life.* By the end, you will have a custom roadmap and step by step plan to get you there from wherever you are now. You will also learn how to change your mindset, a skillset we all need to live our best life.

CHAPTER 2:

But Where Do I Start?

"Whether you think you can or think you can't, you're right."

Henry Ford

Here is the fun exercise I promised to share in Chapter One. If you take it seriously, it can shift your thought process and open an entire world of possibilities for your future. Right now, I know you are thinking, it's just not that simple!" But I am here to tell you "Yes, It Really Is" and I am here to help you do it. I just ask that you genuinely believe that changing your thoughts can change your life. We are all creative beings and if you take this exercise seriously, your mind will provide you with surprising and amazing possibilities. Take some time with it and let your subconscious go to work. It will come up with amazing things.

Step 1: Imagining a Different Life

The foundation for creating the life we want starts with visualization. Human beings are the only creatures on the planet blessed with the gift of imagination. No other creature on the earth has the ability to envision what their future *could be.* Our imagination fuels our creativity and helps us bring forth the things we want in our lives. If we can see it all in our mind's eye first, we can dream it and we can achieve it.

Do not get caught up in the busyness of life, the distractions, and constant demands for our attention. Set aside a time when you can really think about these questions. Think more deeply about your vision, reminisce, reflect, remember moments of joy in your life, let your mind wander and see what comes up for you. Take out a notebook and write down all your responses, thoughts, ideas, and feelings about each question.

1. What would you do if you had all the time and money you needed to do anything you wanted?
2. Where would you put your energy?
3. What do you really want? More importantly, Why?
4. What have you dreamed about doing, being or having?
5. What would you do if you won $50 million in the lottery?
6. How would you invest your newly acquired wealth and time?

Step 2: Your Vision Statement

As children, we daydreamed, and perhaps got in trouble for it. We were told to pay attention, stop wasting time, to be practical. But not now, don't be practical. Daydream and imagine the future believing the life you described in Step 1 is real. Use your notebook again and describe what your life looks like 5 years in the future. If 3 years is easier or resonates with you, use 3 years. Write it down in past tense as if what you describe has already occurred.

1. Where are you living? What does it look like?
2. Who is with you?
3. How are you spending your day?
4. What has happened in the last 5 years?
5. What are you proud of?

Does it sound corny? Maybe. But I am telling you that the process flat out works! It is the reason my husband Tom and I are living our dream life now because many years ago, we created a crystal clear vision of our life as we wanted it to be. We have done it time and time again and I know that you can do it too. I want to pause and share a little of our story as an example of steps 1 and 2.

In 2003, Tom and I chartered a 35-foot sailboat in the British Virgin Islands. We wanted to get married but in order to do so we had to establish a three-day residency, so the honeymoon technically started before the wedding. We were married by the registrar/justice of the peace in the garden of a resort in Cane Garden Bay. It was a magical day in a breathtaking setting. A true technicolor dream. After the ceremony, we were on the beach trying to take pictures of each other and a man walking up the beach offered to take our pictures. He happened to be an artist and took the most incredible pictures of us. Then he handed the digital camera back to us and kept on walking. That night at dinner we set the camera on our table and went dancing. People picked up our camera and took pictures of us. We look back on that day with such joy and fond memories. It was incredible and could not have been better if we had planned it.

After three weeks we had to go back home to Southern California. Leaving the airport, we got on the 405 freeway. There were six lanes of traffic in each direction, and none were moving. We were jolted back to our then current reality of the concrete jungle, the hustle and bustle. With our storybook wedding memories and inspiration for a new life still fresh in our minds, we looked at each other and exclaimed, "This is our life?"

Something had to change. We got to work asking questions, imagining what our life could be and began creating our dream board. Realizing we no longer wished to stay in that environment, we asked ourselves, if we could live anywhere, where would we like to live? Tom said he liked the panhandle of Florida because he was familiar with the area. I was open to the idea, so we took trips there to check it out. In 2005, we invested in two rental homes in Fort Walton Beach but we decided not move there.

Still in Southern California, we systematically remodeled and redecorated our house room by room. We repainted the grey brick tile floor with a warm caramel & white marbled effect with blue sky and clouds on the ceiling like the Caribbean sky.

I painted a beautiful beach sunset scene on a set of white bi-fold doors. Tom repainted our old white wicker furniture in a caramel color and I found some vibrant tropical fabric and sewed new cushion covers. The room was transformed to an inviting Caribbean Beach hotel lobby bar. We had so many great times in that room.

Next, I tackled two white walls that were a blank canvas screaming for a mural. With the vision of Cane Garden Bay, BVI forever imprinted in my mind, I got out our pictures and bought a bunch of mural painting books. It took a few months to paint but the result was spectacular! It WAS our life-sized dream board! It became a constant reminder of our goal. If you cannot live your dream life now, bring some elements of your dream life into your current life.

One day, shortly after we bought our house in Mexico over a decade later, I was admiring the stunning ocean views. I looked north and it hit me like a ton of bricks: I was looking at the IDENTICAL balusters I had painted in my mural in Southern California. They were not on our property; they were our neighbor's, but they were in our ocean view and it was all just like the mural I had painted in our dining room.

Over the years, we have made many more dream boards and have come to notice how many other images and occurrences from those dream boards have made their way into our reality. If you have ever read "The Secret" or watched the movie you know what I mean. The images we hold in our mind, if magnetized with emotion can truly become our reality.

Step 3: The Magnetic Power of Emotion

One of my mentors taught me "the universe loves a made-up mind" and I believe it. So, figure out WHAT you WANT and believe it. For some thinking can be hard. It is easier to simply escape into other distractions and not think about important matters. But you must do the work to make it real. Every little step counts.

The first steps of defining your dream life, are the most important piece of Claiming Your Dream Life. That is why the method to the magic is to start with the result, exactly what you did in Steps 1 and 2. Your vision and 5-year statement are a somewhat clear idea of what you want. I say somewhat because dreams can and will be re-defined and changed as you delve deeper into what really matters. In Chapter 10 we'll cover how this attracts what you want and how to repel the things you don't want in your life.

We are going to go deeply in the process because I want you to get results quickly. If you want a breakthrough, it will happen if you do the work. I have helped people get closer to their dreams and watched as they successfully sharpened their vision and plans to ones that motivated them to quickly live their dream life. Not all at once, but by taking the little steps that turn the big dream into reality.

Obstacles

Think about what might be holding you back from achieving your goal. Take time to really think about these questions.

1. What do you find most challenging,
2. What is holding you back from having your dream life?
3. Are these obstacles real?

Write down your answers and thoughts in your notebook.

The two most common obstacles I find are (1) where do I even start; and (2) what about money and finances? The good news, you have already started and later in this book we will cover finances. By the time you are finished you will have covered all the obstacles and will have developed your complete roadmap. If an obstacle remains, reach out and I will help suggest ways towards a solution.

The Roadmap

Your roadmap will give you actionable steps to move you from where you are now to closer to your dream life. My formula for your success is: Clarity + Focus + Action = Results. Action is a key part of the formula, this can be where good intentions get stuck.

The Law of Inertia simply says a body at rest tends to stay at rest while a body in motion tends to stay in motion. If you are at rest, it is like pushing a car along the road. The hardest part is getting it rolling. Once it gets rolling, the momentum makes it easier and easier to keep going. My intention for you, is to get you rolling so you will keep moving forward. Each chapter builds on the next. So, try to read them in order as the material will make a lot more sense for you.

The Time is Now

Today, more people are worried about the state of affairs, and the economy than any time in the most recent past. People are uncertain and concerned about their future. There is no doubt we are in the midst of historic change but with historic change, comes historic opportunity. There just could not be a better time than NOW to take charge of your future, your life, and your circumstances.

In the first episode of my Overseas Life Redesign podcast, Tom and I have a conversation we call When Life Got Rough, Setting Sail on a Sea of Change. We talk about being devastated by the 2008 financial crash. Tom had a thriving electrical engineering business and it dried up overnight. I was in the business of marketing and selling employee benefits to companies that were now closing their doors or having massive layoffs. Our income shrunk to a fraction of what we had been making. We owned two rental properties plus our own home, all three went into foreclosure. It was an exceedingly difficult period. I know there are many people right now who are struggling. What I have to say is "hang in there," keep hope alive because things do change. They can change very, very rapidly for you. Be ready. Create the vision of what you want, visualize it and take action to make it happen.

A Clear Vision

We have discussed step one in detail, which is the need for Clarity. You need to have a crystal-clear vision of what you want your dream life to look like, then work backward to create it. That means you must think about, and then decide what you want. Once you have done that, only then can you create your step-by-step plan.

Of course, the plan will be different for everyone depending on how simple or complicated your life is, whether you have income that will support you no matter where you live. If you have career, familial or business obligations that will affect your timing. After you create your custom roadmap, then you can develop a step-by-step plan and an implementation Strategy.

Throughout the pages of this book, you will hear many stories about how others have done it. There is no cookie-cutter way to achieve your dream life, but there are a ton of strategies and methods you can model. So, buckle up and enjoy the ride!

Since I started teaching this process, I have had the pleasure of working with people who have made incredible progress in a truly short time. I will share their stories as we get further into the book. What excites me is seeing several clients come in with a five-year plan. One moved within six months and another is moving to Paradise within 14 months of starting the Academy program. Other Dream Lifers have shortened their five-year plans to just two years.

A Step-by-Step Plan

How did they do it? The Roadmap created Clarity about what they wanted. Clarity supplied the insight necessary to know what to Focus on so they could develop a step-by-step plan. Using what they learned they set achievable goals, created checklists, monthly plans and identified the daily activities to implement their plan. The foundational work meant they could focus on taking the right action to make their dream a reality. That is ultimately what led to such fast results. They followed my formula: Clarity + Focus + Action = Results. You can do the same thing by following the steps outlined in this book.

There Will Always Be Trade-Offs

Another universal law I want to bring up here is the Law of Sacrifice. This law states that something must always be sacrificed for something else. Or, as I say: there will always be trade-offs. When we moved to Paradise in 2017, Tom sold his cherished 1971 BMW Motorcycle. I sold my 1996 Nissan 300ZX Convertible, a present to myself after passing the bar. Why? We sold them because they did not fit into our new lives and lifestyle. We parted with other treasures that simply were not compatible with our new life. Do we miss them? Some. Perhaps a little. Was it worth it? Totally.

Fundamental Interests

I want to explain the role of fundamental interests in this process. This is a concept Henry Kissinger used in putting together the famous Middle East peace agreement. He looked at the fundamental interests of the parties involved, what they really wanted and then worked out a compromise that addressed and satisfied all of them. It is the same principle that I want you to consider in the context of moving overseas. I will give you a couple of examples so you can understand what I mean.

In my case, when I met my husband Tom, he lived on a 30-foot sailboat and he went sailing every weekend. He was also an international yacht racer, he practiced or raced three or four times a week. It was a passion that was a particularly important part of his life. He took me sailing on our first date. He wanted to find out if I got seasick and if I did, we were just not going to work. Sailing was a fundamental interest Tom had and fortunately, I passed the test. We both have fundamental interests, and they are complementary. I grew up in Minnesota. and spent a lot of time on the water on powerboats, water skiing and fishing. So, I really took to sailing quite well.

I also had a fundamental interest of my own which I made mine crystal clear to him once things got serious between us. It was my dislike of cold weather and disdain for snow. I told him I did not want to see snow any closer than the snow-peaked mountain tops I could see in the distance when we lived in Orange County. Tom was a Black Diamond expert skier but decided his knees were not that good anymore and would trade Black Diamond runs for tennis and golf.

We have some friends from Minnesota, Pat and Rita. Pat hates the cold, and in Minnesota it gets bitter cold in the winter. So, they come down to Mexico for the winter to get away from the cold. Rita does not care for the heat; the tropics are not her thing as she gets overheated easily. She likes a little bit cooler climate, but she knows how unhappy Pat is in the winter in Minnesota. She is willing to sacrifice a little bit of comfort for three months so Pat can get out of the cold. Even though she might be a little uncomfortable on some of the warmer days, they enjoy their time together. It is a compromise they have that makes them both happy.

You may have other fundamental interests that come into play. One lady said, "Oh, what about the grandchildren?" I thought, well you know you can keep them. You do not have to give up your grandchildren and who knows, maybe they will come visit you more. Or maybe you have other family responsibilities. One friend took care of her mom, who had Alzheimer's for ten years. Unfortunately, the time came when her mom did not recognize her anymore. When it became clear that it really did not matter who was taking care of her mom, my friend felt free to leave. Taking care of her mom was really a fundamental interest that kept her from moving and creating her dream life overseas. Once circumstances changed, while the fundamental interest of having her mom taken care of was still there, she did not need to be the caregiver anymore.

Wherever You Go, There You Are

Changing geographic locations alone will rarely make you happy if you are unhappy in your current location. Instead, it is better to become happy and grateful exactly where you are right now. While getting ready to leave a place you have lived for a long time, I have found joy by focusing on the unique things that will be missed in your new location. For example, downtown Orange, California is charming. It has a traffic circle with a park in the center and it is populated with adorable Craftsman-style homes and some lovely Victorian homes. We knew for more than a year in advance we would be leaving Southern California. Sometimes people feel animosity toward a place (or relationships) when they are "done" with it. Instead, I savored every joyous moment, knowing we would soon be moving on.

Every time I took my downtown Orange walking route, I made it a practice to admire the beautiful homes, both modest and large, the intricate details of the architecture, the unique landscaping, the brilliant flowers, the cats peacefully napping in their favorite spot. As I walked around the downtown plaza traffic circle, I imprinted the charm and quaintness, the restaurants, many antique shops, college kids gathered in the coffee shops. I would soak it all up, taking it in like taking a deep breath, like I would never see it again. It was a community I loved and life I was so very blessed to have. I felt incredibly grateful and a sense of completeness, as if a chapter of my book was closing. Yet I eagerly looked forward to our new life with unknown adventures. While we were "done" with the Southern California rat race, we were not running away from something as much as running toward something else, a more enriched life.

Although we planned to move, we still remodeled our home in Orange, as described earlier. We thoroughly enjoyed being there because we created an environment with decor that spoke to and reminded us daily of our dreams and future. It also would help with resale when the time came. Freedom and happiness come from accepting yourself as you are and then finding a life that suits you and it really is not as difficult as you might think. A common question is "Where do I go?", and that is what I will help you figure out next!

I am committed to changing lives and making dreams come true. It is a bold promise, I know, but I've done it. I can promise that if you go through this process and you do not want to be restricted to where you live, this is for you.

CHAPTER 3:

How to Pick Your Paradise

Urban, Rural or Beach?

Lifestyle

Do you love the hum of a city, the theater and lots of live entertainment options? Then a sleepy village will just not be the best fit for you.

Do white sandy beaches make your heart sing? If so, an urban concrete jungle is not going to be your idea of paradise.

Or do you just not know? Then be adventurous and "try on" different places and environments. Barbara and her husband were unsure so they "tried on" different places until they finally found the perfect fit, their idea of paradise. That's what I call the Goldilocks Method and I'll show you a great example of it a bit later in this chapter.

Activities

When you move to your new place things will not be the same as home. There will be new ways of doing things, new activities, new friends to make, and new opportunities. These may be social, philanthropic, profit producing or just the chance to slow down and relax. What activities are important to you? Being a social butterfly, making a difference for others, or just relaxing on that lounge chair and writing your novel.

Many people retire without a well thought out plan. They neglect to define what their new life will look like each day. Being retired with an income stream is not a plan. It defines your situation but not how you will spend your days. With no structure or purpose people will drift. Without knowing what else to do, some may head to the bar every day or just sit in their new place and wonder why they moved in the first place.

Naming what is important to you at the beginning of your search will help you find and focus on the places that 'fit' your vision of paradise and help you craft a plan for your new life.

Culture

Culture is to a society what personality is to humans. Culture is reflected in the customs, arts, social institutions, and achievements of a particular nation, people, or other social group. Just as there are many variations in the human personality, geographic areas even within a country, have many variations as well. You will inevitably experience culture shock. You can count on it.

Don't forget to investigate the various subcultures or shared interest groups that exist as well. These could be church groups, men's or women's clubs, volunteer or social organizations, expat groups, special interest groups such as theater aficionados and more. There are a wide range of possibilities; some will suit you and others will not.

Even countries like Canada and United States, which seemingly have similar cultures, actually have significant cultural differences. The prevalence of fear is one. While not a huge Michael Moore fan, he has done some interesting work exploring the nature of fear in his documentary called *Bowling for Columbine*, which analyzed the 1999 Colorado high school shooting. In the film, Moore compares the prevalence of guns in the United States to other countries. Canada, for example, has about the same number of firearms as the US. In 2018, Canada had 660 gun homicides, while the US had a staggering 14,000. (CDC)

Moore says the reason for this disparity is because the US is built on a culture of fear. At the birth of the country, it was fear of the British, then it was the Native Americans, then fear of the slaves, whose population greatly exceeded the slave owners. That fear evolved over time spreading to anyone who looked out of place, especially in US suburbs.

In contrast, Canadians do not have this culturally ingrained fear. In the documentary, Moore did an experiment where he'd approach houses in the United States and tested to see if the front door was locked. Of course, all the front doors were locked up like Fort Knox.

Then he goes to Canada, but all their front doors were unlocked. He would just walk into people's homes and the Canadians would just smile and say, "Hello, can I help you?" This is a significant cultural difference between two seemingly similar countries. I'll talk more about fear in a subsequent chapter.

Economy or First Class?

Affordability

Affordability is often the primary reason people move overseas from the United States and Canada. If this is one of the reasons you are contemplating a move overseas, comparing living expenses between 'home' and 'paradise' is one exercise that is an important part of making your plan. If it all seems too good to be true, a short-term "beta test", living like a local, can be the perfect way to find out what the true costs will be before you take the plunge and move completely.

Accessibility

Accessibility will be an essential factor in your plan. There are plenty of beautiful and inexpensive places to live in the world, but just how easy or difficult is it to get to them?

Think about your travel patterns and goals. What are your plans for future travel? Do you travel for work or pleasure? Do you go to a particular place often? Is it relatively easy for your friends and family to visit? If you fly to the airport, do you still have to take a long bus, train, or car ride to get to your new place?

Investigate the airlines, the destinations, and the ease of flying from your home city to your new city. If your new airport is a popular destination, there will be many airlines servicing that route. The cost may be less and most likely, it will be easier to get there from most major cities. One reason we selected Panama City, Florida was because they had just completed a new International Airport. It was lovely but it only attracted two airlines with very limited routes.

One reason we chose to live on Isla Mujeres is that you can fly pretty much anywhere in the world from Cancun. It is about a three-and-a-half-hour flight to Minneapolis, my hometown. Southern California is about 4 hours and Toronto, Canada is just under 4 hours. From our home on the beach, it is an 18-minute ferry ride to mainland Mexico and then a 30-minute taxi or shuttle ride to the Cancún airport.

Healthcare Access

Access to quality healthcare providers is most likely on your "must-have" list included in your plan. Here we are referring to the accessibility of doctors, clinics, and hospitals. Make a list of all your providers so you know which ones you will need to find after you move. Facebook expat groups can be one of the sources you use for information. Once on the ground, you can ask around and find out the quality and proximity of the providers you need.

When we arrived, I asked around and was referred to a chiropractor from Houston, a Dutch chiropractor from Veracruz, Mexico and Dr. Greta, a British general practitioner. I also have a great dentist and an excellent veterinarian. In Chapter 5, we will discuss the delivery and cost of healthcare.

Community

In the USA, individuality is an important societal value. People there are more likely to prioritize self-interest over the interest of the entire community. This differs greatly from the importance of community and the common good in other cultures around the world. When you evaluate the culture of a community, consider what values the people of the community embrace. Do you share those same values? Do you want to be part of a caring, local community? Would you be more comfortable in a gated expat community? Figuring out your values will help you decide which will work best for you.

We love living on Isla because the concept of community is fully embraced. We see deep multigenerational relationships where family members of all ages work together, play together and often live together. Our community is dependent on tourism for its livelihood. No tourists, no income. When need arises, the whole community, including expats, comes together to help each other by doing what it takes. In a recent economic crisis, my friend, Brenda, helped raise money to buy diapers, formula, and groceries every single day. All delivered with the help of a good Samaritan taxi driver.

Are you a born organizer building tribes and connecting people with similar interests? My friend Tiffany Lanier started The Sisters of Perpetual Disorder as a social support group for single females living on the island. It has grown and evolved through the years to become a terrific go-to resource for anything we and the community needs. You'll enjoy her story a little later.

Climate

Weather is an important consideration. How would you describe the weather in your paradise? Add your desired weather to your plan. If you do not like tropical weather, you probably do not want to go to the Caribbean. Think about the activities you most enjoy and the weather that goes with them. If you love to ski you would probably want to be close enough to someplace where you could go skiing.

For me, I would be happy if I never see the snow again. Everybody is different. You will have to decide what is important to you.

Safety

Safety is always a consideration. I often laugh when I hear comments people make, "Is it safe in Mexico?" Mexico is a great big country and there are all kinds of cities and villages of different sizes. There are large areas with literally no people. It is sort of like asking, "Is the United States safe?" In any country we know there are safer areas and there are places where it is not a good idea to go, particularly after dark.

The local area where you will actually live is more meaningful than how safe the country is as a whole. This is not to say that some countries do not have national safety issues. Safety is a consideration that should be part of your plan and something you will have to research.

Language

If you do not want to learn a different language, and want to speak only English, then Belize, just south of Mexico, might be a good fit. If English is a requirement for you, then your search should include English-speaking countries. If you plan to move to an area with a tourist-based economy you might get along well speaking just English. Research has shown that learning a new language helps keep you young and stimulates your brain.

Spanish is an easy language to learn. Isla Mujeres is very tourist driven and many people do speak English. While you might want to live somewhere that isn't a tourist spot, the prevalence of English might make a touristy area attractive to you. There are many options for learning new languages, apps, Google translate and more. There are also areas where there is no native language but in fact multiple languages spoken by many for example Greece and Switzerland. Learning at least a little of the local language and trying to communicate using it is a sign of respect.

Test the waters before taking the plunge

Aside from the accessibility of Mexico from the US or Canada, another benefit has been the ease of getting a long term visa. Mexico routinely granted a six month tourist visa when entering the country. This custom has historically been a hassle free way to legally remain in Mexico for half the year. Many snowbirds stay in Mexico for the winter months annually, including property owners not wanting the hassle or expense of applying for temporary or permanent legal residency.

Some people elect to leave the country after six months and then return just a short time later, thereby obtaining a new six month tourist visa. There have been reports that Mexico may be ending this customary practice. Computerized immigration processing means the immigration authorities now can easily verify visitor travel patterns. An automatic 180 day visitor visa is no longer guaranteed when entering Mexico, particularly when regular 180 day stays are revealed in the records.

All foreign citizens traveling to Mexico must fill out an Official Entry Immigration Form (FMM) prior to their arrival to Mexico. To ease the immigration entry process you can fill out the Immigration Form(s) online in the comfort of your home or office. The registration process is very convenient and straightforward and all you need is your passport, flight information, address or name of the hotel where you are staying.

A visitor visa allows you to stay in Mexico for a period of up to 180 days, provided that you are not carrying out any paid activities. This includes tourism, volunteering, studying courses shorter than six months, transit, and attending business meetings provided no monetary earnings will be derived from your activities in Mexico.

Take A Sabbatical

What if you really don't know what you want or where you want to live? You might try taking a one year sabbatical and "try on" different locations and lifestyles. Theresa Stark found a company that offered a one-year discover the world program. The company made all the arrangements for her. All Teresa had to do was show up in Mexico City, the first city on the program calendar. She stayed for a month and then every month for a year she moved to a different city in the world!

As a teenager, Chris Pordon became inspired after reading *The Four Hour Work Week* by Tim Ferris. In his late 20's, while appearing to live a good life with a great job in New York City, Chris was dissatisfied with both his career and lifestyle. A random conversation at a party about picking up and going off to travel the world stuck with him. A few months later, he quit his job, moved out of his apartment and broke up with his girlfriend. He booked a one-way flight to London, and didn't return from Europe for two years.

When his funds began to run out, he looked for remote work so he could continue traveling. He found a surprisingly long list of such opportunities online. Many American companies are looking to leverage the lower cost of living in other cities, states and even other countries. They want a remote workforce with a lower cost, and Chris says he won the digital nomad lottery with his first company. He has never looked back and is now living "sustainably homeless" as his mom refers to his lifestyle.

Grow Your Bank Account by House Sitting

Our Canadian neighbors, who lived on their boat in the slip next to ours, spent six glorious months living in the magical city of Merida, Mexico for free. They were house sitters for snow-birds who returned north and wanted their lovely large pool home with gardens cared for. Our friends had grown weary of how slow and crowded the Cancun Immigration Office was so decided to move to Merida long enough to get their permanent residency application processed and approved.

Their plan was to rent an apartment, when a terrific house sitting opportunity came along. As a result, they got a much bigger and nicer place to live and were only asked to pay for utilities. Their cat Kokomo moved in too. They found this awe-some opportunity through a Facebook House Sitting Group. No money was exchanged for their services.

House sitting has been around for many years. When we transited the Panama Canal in 2010, a couple who crewed with us had just finished a house sitting stint in Costa Rica. House sitting is becoming increasingly popular which means more opportunities for both sitters and homeowners.

House sitters can experience different cultures and locations in a budget friendly manner. Homeowners can travel with peace of mind and not worry about leaving their homes and pets behind. You can meet new people, enjoy new places and like our retired Canadian friends, stay in a much nicer place than they would otherwise have been able to afford.

It is a great way to to check out an area before moving there. For a digital nomad like Chris, house sitting is a very smart strategy: a way to work, see new places and save money all at the same time. It is also a good option to consider if you have a strong desire to travel on a budget or want an inexpensive way to scout out potential places to live.

In his early sixties, George White changed coasts and moved from Florida where he had lived for over thirty years to California. After six years in Southern California he knew he wanted to travel and started researching house sitting. In July of 2018, he took a leap of faith and started house sitting. In 2020 George was a guest on my podcast. When we spoke, he was in Italy, just north of Rome. He explained that he really enjoyed house sitting, watering plants, and cuddling animals. It really keeps his expenses low because rent, mortgage and car expenses have been completely removed from his budget. When I spoke to George, he told me his bank account balances had doubled during the few short years he'd been house sitting.

At age 71, the retired radio host still works as a voice actor. He has regular clients in Florida and in the Carolinas. They always ask him "Where are you now, George?" His reply might be that he's in Sorrento, Italy looking at Mount Vesuvius across the Bay of Napoli while recording their project. They tell George they want to be like him when they grow up.

The Goldilocks Method

When Barbara Harris and her husband left Canada, they had a specific plan for finding their paradise. They envisioned being part of a Mexican community, so their plan included studying Spanish so that they would be able to communicate with the people they met along the way. Their plan also called for them to downsize from a big house to a two-bedroom condo before they began the drive from Canada to Mexico.

They owned a timeshare, so they researched and found eight units available in the interior of Mexico all within driving distance. The two senior citizens hit the road in a big old gray van with Canadian license plates and driver's licenses. They spent a week in each location, driving from place to place. The only trouble was a flat tire that cost about five Canadian dollars plus a 20-peso tip ($1USD) to repair. Barbara says they did not run into any trouble because they do not attract that sort of thing into their life. Always trust your gut.

At first, they lived in Puerto Morelos, an adorable beach town halfway between Cancun and Playa del Carmen. They loved it there, but it is a small town. Other towns they considered were too big and touristy, they wanted something in between. One rainy day they saw an episode of House Hunters International and learned about Merida. They rented a car for a week and lined up a realtor who showed them beautiful colonial homes in Mérida, which were extremely affordable.

They loved Merida, but had just moved from the hustle and bustle, buses, and busy streets of Vancouver, British Columbia and were not interested in any more hustle and bustle. They decided to check out Progresso, a beach area about a half-hour drive north of Merida, to look at a few homes there. As they drove back to Merida, Barbara told her husband they could afford the last villa they saw. She had figured it all out in her head, knowing exactly how much their income and expenses were. She calculated they could retire early in Progresso if they went back to Canada and sold everything. They went to bed in the hotel that night and when Barbara woke up the next morning, her husband said, "You know, you're right!" He pulled up his fancy spreadsheets on the computer and showed her that they even had $100 a month to spare.

They called their realtor in Canada and said, "sell it." They made an offer on a Progresso villa one block from the beach and seven months later, they packed up in Canada and moved to their beautiful, fully furnished, two bedrooms, two bath villa with a private swimming pool for $140,000 CAD!

They made many amazing friends and never spent the holidays alone. If they were sick, friends showed up with dinner or whatever else they needed. Progresso is a very flat beach town and after four years, her husband longed for mountains and scenic ocean views. Although they both loved being near the ocean, they decided to try somewhere more scenic. They rented a house in a gated community called Los Arroyos about 10 minutes from the ocean, where they stayed for five months.

Barbara dreamed of living in a cute, quaint little, small Mexican town instead of a gated community. While at a dinner party they met a man, who owned a house in a little town called La Desembocada, about fifteen minutes southeast of Puerto Vallarta. It was a big house with great outdoor space. The rent was $600 CAD per month. They stayed there for seven months, but her vision of a cute little Mexican town did not match the town.

In reality, the town was way too little. Less than 1,000 people lived there which meant there were limited amenities, services, and little ability to integrate or make friends in the community. So even though it was a good-sized home with nice outdoor space at a great price, they found themselves going into town to visit friends at least four or five days a week.

One day they saw an ad for a two-bedroom, two-bath, condo with vaulted ceilings that overlooked a golf course on the third floor. They jumped on it. Their realtor recommended a contractor to redo the kitchen. They went overboard with the remodel, even installing a built-in cement bathtub, which Barbara always wanted, with little glass, sparkly tiles. It was stunning when it was finished. Living on the third floor with no elevator became challenging when Barbara developed health issues and hip problems. They sold the condo and moved back to Los Arroyos.

The Los Arroyos gated community was a fallback place and not really their cup of tea. One day, Barbara was on Facebook and saw a great property. It had been a mango farm owned by a couple with seven kids. The dad died young, leaving his wife with seven children. They continued to run the mango farm and any extra money they had was used to buy more land. The property was eventually subdivided into 20 good-sized lots. Now Canadians, Americans, Mexicans and one Italian have bought lots and built wonderful homes. Barbara and her husband rented the last home owned by the original owner. It is still a gated development, but it suits their lifestyle a lot better.

They positively love the home and the location. It takes one minute to get to the main road, then in six minutes, they are at the beach. They can park right there and walk the beach or be at two or three restaurants within a couple of minutes. It is just a ten-minute drive to three major grocery stores that have everything she wants. Goldilocks finally found her paradise. A place that's 'Just Right'.

The lesson in the story is to be flexible, don't be afraid to try on different locations, lifestyles and climates until you find one that is the perfect fit.

Chapter Exercise:

Write a description of your perfect day in paradise. Be specific and use all five of your senses to make it real. Pretend you have just won the lottery; you can do anything you want to do. How will you spend your time?

Where are you? How does the earth feel under your feet? What do you smell? Do you smell salt in the air or maybe a favorite dish cooking? What do you hear? What are the sounds? Waves crashing, the birds singing, music from a particular region, a specific instrument, a different language. What is the climate? Engage all five senses as you complete the exercise.

What are you going to do after you wake up? Do you wake to an alarm clock? Do you meditate? Exercise? Going for a walk? What are you having for breakfast? What are you doing after that?

What activities are you doing? What will you work on? Do you want to write a book? Paint? Create? Describe activities that really light you up?

The more you engage all your senses, the more real the vision will become and the more emotion you will attach to it. Emotion is the secret sauce that magnetizes and accelerates the entire process of moving your dream life closer to you.

In the next chapter, we will explore how you can use the power of your mind to Claim Your Dream Life in Paradise.

CHAPTER 4:

A Gift of Twice the Time

In 1860 life expectancy was age 40, now it is 80 and projected to be 85 by 2050. There is also an exponentially-growing number of us living to age 100. This dramatic lengthening of our lifetime is a beautiful gift. Over the past century, there have been three age-related stages of life, learn, earn, retire.

We learn until our mid-20s by going to college or learning a craft or skill in a job. Then we earn for about four decades with a job. To retire meant to no longer work. This final stage historically only lasted about 10 years so not much effort went into planning this final stage. Today we continue to learn throughout our entire lifetimes. We can also continue to earn by working remotely from all parts of the world and working for ourselves.

Redefining Retirement

In midlife and retirement, what we experience today differs greatly from what our parents and grandparents experienced. We are living longer and have more time but lack a roadmap of possibilities and are on our own to try to navigate all of this.

Aside from some physical health and job performance support, we are not well prepared or supported for this period of life. There is not a clearly defined set of rules, expectations, or responsibilities. Life has changed for everyone.

Retiring used to mean you no longer had to go to work. Today many who are 'retired' are still working either by necessity or by choice. Also, out of necessity, they are caring for their parents and elderly relatives, helping the younger generations get established, lending a hand if there is an unexpected job loss or helping with the kids or childcare expenses. Many transitions we experience in midlife, and are mostly unprepared for, can become overwhelming and disorienting to us.

Retirement is being completely redefined. It is not the beginning of the end or simply continuing the life we had before. While there may be a short period of rest and relaxation, most people want much more. In fact, today's retirees view retirement as a new chapter in life, the next adventure. To be sure, retirees do gain some freedom: from work stress, commuting and office drama. The pressures of working and raising a family have passed but other stressors can appear or remain. According to The Federal Reserve, among households ages 45-54, a staggering 42% have no retirement savings and the median retirement savings is less than $100,000.

Stereotypes of what this stage of life is like are inaccurate and not helpful. Studies published by AARP show negative portrayal of adults 50-plus is more common than negative portrayal of younger adults. While this group comprises 51% of consumer buying power and 45% of the population, they are severely underrepresented on both the big screen and on television. When older adults are represented, they are seven times more likely to be portrayed negatively than younger adults. Instead of depicting older adults as positive and happy, retirees are often stereotyped as out of touch, technologically incompetent and dependent. These stereotypical messages make it more difficult for this demographic to imagine the inspired possibilities for their next chapter of life.

The truth is, ageism abounds in the United States culture which values youth. There's an obvious bias against older people, and some have called it the last socially acceptable prejudice. At what specific age do we become "old" anyway? Middle age (which *was* "old" in the last century) can be a very difficult period to navigate. This "Middlescense" period (from adulthood to old age - similar to adolescence as the transition from childhood to adulthood) is in the process of being completely redefined. It is a four decade long period of time, and we haven't been given the tools or the training necessary to navigate the frequent life transitions we experience during this period of our life.

None of us receive a manual to guide us through this challenging period of life, nor is there any sort of rite of passage initiation. We are on our own to keep learning and growing so that we may thrive in these times of constant and rapid change. We don't want to just live a longer life, we want to be living longer as a healthier, happier, member of society with the freedom to make our own choices and chart a course toward our desired future.

Mindset Matters

Research shows that older people with a positive mindset on aging, who feel worthy, happy, and hopeful as they get older, lived seven and a half years longer than those with a negative perspective about aging. My husband is 10 years older than me. Sometimes he will make a comment about being old and I will say, "Oh no, you're not. Don't say that!" I encourage you to catch yourself when you get stuck in these outdated ruts about how we view ourselves.

One of the intangible benefits of living overseas I have heard repeatedly from my podcast guests is feeling young and alive. This wonderful feeling of being vibrant and youthful is one reason we moved here. Before that, we lived in a much older community in Florida. The vibrancy in that culture was lacking. It was not a good 'fit' for us.

Being in a totally new and foreign environment is an exciting adventure. Think back about going to your first state fair or maybe on your first exotic vacation or another life experience that left a big impression on you. Recall the sense of wonder, the sense of joy of exploring new places, having experiences you never had before. Remember the sense of adventure, new discoveries, the wonder of it all, and imagine feeling that again, feeling young and totally alive once again. What is that worth?

Purpose Provides Meaning

If we chose it we have a blank slate, a fresh canvas to design the next phase of our life. We can stay the same or do something completely different. Cliff Holmes was raised on a cattle and dairy farm in very rural Missouri. There were 28 kids in his graduating class. He left behind life on the farm at 17 years old. He went to college, graduated with a degree in accounting and worked as an accountant until age 39.

Over the years he smartly invested in real estate and stocks. He started investing in real estate, buying up small parcels of farmland; 40 acres, 80 acres, 107 acres, 500 acres. He would combine the parcels to create larger ranches. By the time he left his accounting job, Cliff was earning more from his businesses than what he was offered to become an accounting firm partner. Preparing tax returns for other farmers revealed which farms were profitable and those that were not.

A few decades ago, Cliff learned about holistic farm management from a South African man and started applying those concepts in his farm business. People started to take notice of his success and wanted to know more. He was invited to write articles for agricultural periodicals, and at one point, he was writing a column in four different magazines every single month. Then he was asked to write a book on the subject, which was published under the pen name Cody Holmes. His first book, *Ranching Full-Time on Three Hours a Day: Real-World Validation of Holistic Systems for Stockmen*, was published by Acres U.S.A., Inc. in 2011.

Cliff believes success in farming can't be bought. It must be built and practiced like a law or medical practice. Planning, decision making and wisdom are essential ingredients to success. His own personal successes and failures are all laid bare in his book, to teach the important principals. His timing could not have been better, Cliff's book was published the same year the World Wildlife Fund launched their Sustainable Ranching Initiative.

The blossoming of interest in this field led to Cliff's next career as an author and speaker. Strong demand for his expertise meant book signings, presentations, and speaking engagements all over the country. Along the way, he realized he was a workaholic and after a surprise divorce he decided to make some serious changes. He liquidated his businesses and set off to travel the world.

Although financially able to go first class, he travelled like a college kid. He toured Latin America with just a backpack and jumped on the chicken bus to go from hostel to hostel. He got a call from his friend Ray, a third generation leader of a humanitarian project in Southeast Asia, to come visit. Cliff jumped on a plane from Latin America and landed in Myanmar, where he stayed for a month to work at an orphanage.

Afterwards, he traveled all over Southeast Asia, learning from much younger, more experienced travelers doing the same thing. He visited the killing fields in Cambodia, which he emotionally described as jabbing a knife in his heart. The trip to Southeast Asia changed him. He decided at age 60, with all of his business success, it was time for him to do some good in the world. Cliff has learned to slow down and relax, while enjoying the process of writing his next book.

The Soul did not come here to Retire

I want to share another story with you about my friend Peggy's experience with retirement. She and her husband live in the Upper Midwest, and her husband, Larry, is a retired firefighter. They started coming down to Mexico for vacation in the winter. At first they would come for a week, then a couple of weeks, a month and then it was for a couple of months. The reason, she said, was because Larry could not stand the trauma of the winter. If you have ever lived in a cold climate, you may be familiar with winter depression. It's real and many suicides are a result of winter depression.

To get away from the cold and this gruesome time of year as a first responder, Peggy and Larry would come to an island oasis. He was content to sit and look out at the ocean. She was a retired physical therapist and she got bored just sitting around. So, Peggy started doing some volunteer work and quickly noticed the local artisans were losing sales because they could not speak English. As the island became popular, more and more tourists were coming. She saw a need and opened an English school. Peggy had no background in education, teaching English or any other language. She simply saw a need and decided to address it.

She operated the school for many, many years and it had a huge positive impact on the local community. Peggy eventually got burned out when the school became all-consuming. Over the years, the need for it lessened, because the public schools started teaching English. When the school closed Peggy and Larry repurposed the building into a residential rental.

After that, Peggy started a university scholarship program for locals. It now funds about 10 or 12 young adults per year who are financially supported by 100 donors. They are organized into teams: Team Eduardo, Team Maria, etc., and the donors and their students correspond with each other. The donors support these young adults through college, which is not expensive in Mexico. Tuition and room and board is a small fraction compared to what it costs in the United States. But it is a lot of money to them.

Donors chip in fifty or a hundred bucks a month to help support the student, whose team they're a part of. So, this is what she has done in her retirement. Peggy keeps busy. As I always say, the soul did not come here to retire. Some people do long to retire, and I understand the desire to stop working. I love working with people wanting something more. They want to leave a legacy. They want to make an impact. I think (and the research proves) that having a purpose is really what brings us joy. I know that makes my life rich when I can help others to find their purpose. Retirement does not provide that.

Stress Reduction

One of the intangible benefits of moving overseas that I have experienced, and I hear repeatedly from others is stress reduction.

When we were living in Southern California I remember canceling the daily newspaper because every morning it was breakfast and bombings. Just seeing the front page of the newspaper became too depressing. We cancelled our subscription and began the first 30 minutes of each day by reading a good book. That small change in our morning routine was life-changing and is one of the reasons we live the life we do today. We stopped focusing on the negative news of the day.

Shifting the focus from negative to a positive can quite literally result in feeling the stress leave your body. When you disengage from the negativity, you will be attracted to communities of people who have also turned their backs on the noise and negativity. Imagine spending your time meeting new people with interesting backgrounds, fascinating stories to share, wisdom about places you should see, experiences you might enjoy. Engaging with people who are more relaxed and living life on their own terms because they have proactively taken steps to live the life they want.

Mastering Your Mind:The Power of Our Thoughts

Our thoughts determine what actions we take, and our actions determine the results that show up in our life. Experts say on average we have between 70,000 to 90,000 thoughts a day! Of those thoughts, 95% are subconscious, and 90% are repetitive. On top of that, 70% of those thoughts are negative. That means we have the same negative subconscious thoughts repeating every day. If we want to implement real, lasting changes, we must learn to control at least some of these subconscious, negative, repetitive thoughts.

To change our life, we must also learn to get control of our emotions since emotions are the language our subconscious mind understands. If you understand what is happening in your body physically, emotionally, and energetically, it is my belief that adopting the necessary thoughts and behaviors will be much easier for you and prove to be much more effective in the long term. Since emotions are a result of our thoughts, changing our thoughts will control our emotions. While not easy the process is straightforward and fairly simple.

It is well known that the brain has several states, and some are more conducive to helping us make the changes we want than others. Theta and Alpha are the two most programmable states while Beta is the state that is the least programmable.

BETA		**Alert** Engaged in Work 'Busy' Thinking
ALPHA		**Relaxed** Images & Visuals Self-Introspection Day Dreaming
THETA		**Between Awake/ Sleep** Deep Meditation Flow of Ideas/ Creativity Altered States
DELTA		**Unconsious** Very Deep Sleep

Before moving on, let's go over how our original operating system gets installed in the first place. When we are young, our brain essentially acts as a video recorder. Before puberty, humans read energy and emotions as opposed to hearing and comprehending the "words" that you say. For those of you who are parents, if you have ever experienced your child "not listening" to you, now you know why. They are listening but they are hearing your emotion and feeling your energy.

If you are a parent, please be keenly aware that HOW you talk to your child is far more important than the WORDS you use. They are picking up your emotions (hopefully love) and reading your energy. It is all being recorded for future reference and it is being stored in the subconscious mind. Those recordings become the source of our self-image. If you are familiar with the phrase "he's just like his dad" now you know why! The son is simply modeling the behavior that was recorded and stored in his subconscious much earlier in his life.

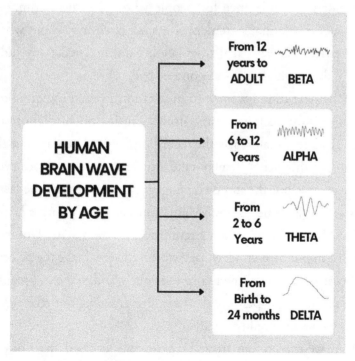

Experts estimate 90% of our limiting beliefs are imprinted in our operating system by age 12. We probably do not even remember when or how our limiting beliefs came to be, as the images we saw and the emotions we experienced were simply being "recorded." Beliefs are merely our thoughts repeated over and over until they become hard-wired patterns. Our beliefs are created at the subconscious level. If we want to understand and/ or change them we must consciously bring them into focus. If we spend time in the Alpha and Theta states, we may actually be able to "see" the recording that is the root of a particular belief.

I had such an experience while in the early stage of creating my program. I had a conversation with a business coach about the type of clients I want to work with. I stated that I have an extremely low tolerance for people who "play the victim." As soon as I made that statement, I got super curious about where that particular value had originated. I did not make any judgment about whether it was good or bad.

The next time I went into meditation I posed the question, "Where is this feeling coming from?" During my mediation session, I quite literally "saw the recording," and I knew at once the source of this belief. It may take a little patience and perseverance at first, but the more you engage in this practice, the faster answers will come to you. Mediation has such positive health effects because it takes our brain into the Theta state. Unfortunately, in our busy modern-day world, too few make it a priority in their lives to take meditation seriously and make it a regular part of their daily practice. Perhaps after learning this technique, you will be inspired to try it.

As we mature our frontal cortex, the "evolved" part of our brain, develops. There is a communication gap between our frontal cortex and our primal or reptilian brain. While our evolved brain is capable of fully distinguishing between social isolation and loneliness versus "real threats" (like being attacked by a wild animal) our reptilian brain cannot. It has only ONE response and the way it communicates is by releasing hormones.

Fortunately, we have the ability to control this chemical response once we learn to speak the language of our subconscious. Our subconscious does not know the difference between a real experience and a vividly imagined experience. That means it is possible to reprogram our software (subconscious) using visualization techniques and our imagination.

As we grow and develop, our personality also evolves, and we become individualized. The ego develops which drives our self-image. In *Your Sacred Self,* Wayne Dyer identifies 6 attributes of the ego: 1) what we have (possessions); 2) what we do (achievements); 3) what others think of us (reputation); 4) we are separate from others (our body means we are "alone"); 5) we are separate from what we lack (disconnected); and 6) we are separate from god/universe.

Dyer says that our ego is the reason we stay disconnected from the creative energy field and cannot create what we want. Our programming as children plays a fundamental role in ego development. Letting go of the ego attributes described above allows you to turn up the volume on your creative energy and decrease resistance to getting what you want.

As a teenager, I was very strong-willed. My father liked to pick verbal fights with me and inevitably I was drawn into an argument with him. It was not pleasant and often ended in bad feelings. One day I had an epiphany, if I just stopped arguing with him, he could not continue. No matter what he said to pick a fight with me, I would just agree with him. At first, it drove him nuts, he would say the most outrageous things to draw me in. I just kept agreeing with him. Eventually, he stopped! Our argument dance was over because I refused to take part. I put my ego in check, and decided it was unnecessary to try to "win" arguments with him.

Have you ever argued with yourself? Ever hear two "voices" at odds with each other, each with a different opinion about what you should be, do or have? This is a conversation between your ego and your higher self. We may not even be aware of it. Paying attention to your inner voices and dialog reveals thoughts and beliefs that may be holding you back. To reprogram your subconscious, it is helpful to gain clarity around the messaging from your existing programming.

Getting control of our thoughts is critical because the only way the subconscious responds is by releasing chemicals (hormones) that are received by all the cells in our bodies either good or harmful ones. If we repeat thought patterns that induce anxiety, fear, stress and overwhelm our hypothalamus releases "fight or flight" chemicals. In an emergency, these can be good chemicals. However, having a mental state under constant stress is very damaging. We can become "addicted" to our own harmful brain chemicals. It is one reason it can be difficult to implement changes in our life. Negative thoughts are the main reason people are not happy and unable to reach their true potential.

It can be hard, if not impossible, to change our thoughts and behaviors, especially as we get older. Information alone is not the answer. If it were, people could simply read a book and lose weight or quit smoking or make any other change they want.

Merely reading the book does not create change. We need to remember that we are hardwired to act in certain ways and our human instincts will inevitably fight us every step of the way. Our instincts are very strong, and their purpose is to keep us safe by preserving the status quo. The way to overcome these evolutionary tendencies and make positive changes in our life is by adopting a system of personal management.

Conquering Your Fears

Fear exists is to protect us. Our biological response to fear is "fight or flight." However, fear is an emotion, which comes from our thoughts. If we can change our thoughts, we can change our emotions. Fear of the unknown is also known as irrational fear, but it can still trigger the same hormonal responses as fear that is rational, that is when there is an identifiable reason for the fear. Another aspect of irrational fear, caused by negative thinking is worry.

A research study about learned helplessness was performed using three groups of rats. They planted mild cancer cells on all of them and knew on average there was a 50% mortality rate under normal circumstances. The first group of rats got mild shocks, but they could learn to avoid them. The group with the ability to control their environment had a 70 percent survival rate! The second group of rats received unavoidable shocks. Their survival rate was only 27 percent, so much lower than 50 percent. This group had learned that is was helpless in avoiding shocks, which caused their much lower survival rate. Group three received no shocks, and their survival rate was 50 percent just as expected.

Other studies show if you feel like you are in control, your chances of living longer go up. If we feel helpless in a situation, it is not good for our survival. Now, make no mistake, there is a big difference between caution and fear. Right? It is smart to be cautious. The key takeaway is that fear is an emotion, which results from thought. And so, it is important to understand it is our underlying thoughts that cause emotion. No one can make us feel a certain way. We choose how we will feel by our thoughts. If you change your thoughts, you can change your feelings.

Fear of the Unknown

To address fear of the unknown when moving overseas, there are simple solutions. You can remove fear and doubt and take the guesswork out of the process with concrete actionable steps. How? Do your research and eliminate the fear of moving by doing a beta test or trial run. I've already talked about testing the waters before you take the big plunge. Rent, do not buy a place right away when you move. We rented for six years while living in Florida because we were not sure if that location would be a good fit. We were glad we did not buy and were free to move on to another destination, unencumbered by real estate. It is perfectly ok to try out different places to see if you like it there, if you don't then simply move on.

Fear of Failure

What would you do if you could not fail?. I love that question! Why are we afraid of failing? Perhaps those old tapes are playing in our head that need to be named and purged. Fear can prevent us from moving forward because we are afraid of making a mistake. If I do not make a move or a decision, then I can't make a mistake.

But that logic does not consider that by doing nothing, we are making a move to preserve the status quo. We are consciously deciding not to have new experiences or to learn new lessons. Saying "no" to those experiences or lessons means we deprive ourselves of the gift of confidence that we receive by reaching our goals. We deny ourselves the ability to see ourself as a winner, someone who sets a goal and achieves it!

Someday Islers is what I used to call people who live a life saying "someday I'll write, someday I'll paint, someday I'll learn how to sail or fly, someday I'll..." Sadly, the graveyards and cemeteries are filled with Someday Islers who left this earth with unfulfilled dreams and aspirations. I hope that is not you.

When you dream and create a vision of your new life overseas and achieve that goal, your total opinion of yourself changes. You achieved a big goal. You can say "I Did It! I Did It! And when you do it once, you gain the confidence to do it again and again. You are not afraid to act. You are a Winner not a Someday Isler.

Remember it is ok if your plans do not work out. What is the worst outcome that could happen if you fail? Perhaps it simply means returning to your old way of life.

Becky and Corky were both librarians who retired in 2016 and moved to Mexico. A few months later Becky's brother got sick, so they returned to the U.S. to take care of him until he passed away. Then in 2018 they decided to try it again. They absolutely loved living on the island of Isla Mujeres, Mexico, but for some reason, it made Becky physically sick. Perhaps it was the heat or humidity or some sort of allergy, but whatever it was it made it impossible for them to stay. They moved back to Missouri and picked up their lives where they had left off. Are they sorry? Not one bit. They went for it, and it did not work out, but they are not left wondering what it might have been like.

Embracing Fear

Courageous people do not lack fear, they have just learned how to manage their emotions and discern the difference between fear and danger. By replacing fear of the unknown with curiosity, we open ourselves up to an infinite stream of possibilities We can let our fear rule our lives or we can become childlike and see endless possibilities, cultivate curiosity, push our boundaries, leap out of our comfort zones, and accept and thrive regardless of what life throws at us. We can change our mindset to one of possibilities.

More on that to come.

CHAPTER 5:

Dispelling Myths and Obliterating Obstacles

Myth #1: It's too expensive, I can't afford it.

Live like a Millionaire for 50% less

If she lived in the U.S. making $100,000 or more a year, Becca Alvarez could have a nice car, live in a nice place and essentially be living paycheck to paycheck. As a single mother raising daughters that was not what she wanted. Her employer offered her the chance to work remotely, so Becca decided to move to Mexico. Here her family can live as if they were millionaires with the same US salary. She can put her daughters in private schools, take two, three, or four vacations a year and have full-time help managing the household. They live in Michoacán, in an area with mountains, trees, lakes, and volcanoes where the climate is a gorgeous, seventy-four degrees year-round. She says it is just like living in Southern California, but at one-tenth of the cost.

Becca says everyone always asks her if she feels safe. She laughs and says she actually feels safer in Mexico than she does in the US. After living in Mexico for one year, they moved to a new suburb in Franklin, Tennessee, where all the homes were worth around $400K. On their first night in the home, with everything still in boxes, she and her girls went to dinner. When they returned, the home had been broken into and the only thing stolen were two little baby turtles they had worked so hard to bring back from Mexico. She thinks it was just some neighborhood kids that broke in and took the turtles. Becca says nothing like that has ever happened to her in Mexico. After one year in Tennessee, they returned to live in Mexico.

Becca was so fearful of child abduction in the United States that she would never let her two and four-year-olds play out in the yard by themselves. Never, ever. In fact, she knows of no parents in the U.S. who would let their children play in a front yard by themselves anymore, even at five or six years old. In Mexico she is not concerned about that at all. She loves that children can run around her town just like they used to fifty years ago in the United States. Now that her girls are older, they walk from their neighborhood into downtown Patzcuaro during the day and take taxis by themselves to return home.

How much does this lifestyle cost Becca? Rent for their four-bedroom home is $300 a month. She moved to Mexico with no furniture because it would cost more to move her furniture than to buy custom made furniture in her new city. Becca showed pictures of pieces she liked from Pinterest to the carpenter who made them for pennies on the dollar.

Four full-time employees manage their household. Because Becca travels for business, her right-hand gal, Clementina, runs everything. She does all the menu planning, grocery shopping, cooking, laundry, ironing and works five days a week from eight until four. Becca employs a full-time nanny for her 3-year-old toddler. A part-time housekeeper cleans the house seven days a week for $60. The yard is about two and a half acres of land, so she has a full-time gardener. He is the young adult son of Clementina and does all the gardening. He is also a handyman that takes care of anything that breaks in the house and if her car needs repairs he takes it to the mechanic.

Becca's job is intense, and she works from eight until six or seven at night, sometimes on weekends, so she does not have time to do anything domestic. When she does stop working, her focus is on spending time with her daughters. It is such a gift. Moms in the US, even those that are well paid, are doing everything. Perhaps they have someone clean once a week or at most twice a week, some only once per month. They are trying to prepare the meals, do the shopping, laundry, homework with the kids and hold together their families while working full-time jobs. The stress of moms in the US is off the charts. By living in Mexico, Becca has been able to reduce her stress, not live paycheck to paycheck, send her daughters to private school and take three to four vacations a year. Becca and her family's quality of life in Mexico is so much better than it could ever be living in the States, especially as a single mom.

Earn Dollars, Spend Pesos

When Cindy Lu's marriage fell apart, she took a vacation to Isla Mujeres to clear her head. Like many, she fell in love with the island on her first trip. She came to the realization that there was nothing for her back in Malibu, California. Cindy is very spiritual and talks to the land. During her talk with the land, she explained if the island wanted her to stay, certain things had to happen, or it would not be possible for her to stay. She made a little "must-have" list and shortly after everything on her list showed up. She had the feeling that life was just leading her. She had been feeling adrift, like she had lost control of the wheel. Cindy no longer felt in alignment with anything in California. But something clicked on the island.

Twelve years earlier, Cindy experienced major health issues that turned out to be black mold toxicity. Western medicine was not able to help her. Her condition was misdiagnosed, and the suggested treatments and prescriptions had made it worse. As a result, she turned to natural wellness solutions. She wanted to learn how to heal herself. Essential oils helped her, so she earned her certification as an international aroma therapist to gain more knowledge. In the end, she built a business around helping others by sharing what she had learned.

In California, she created the oil blends and sold them to her clients. When she decided to move overseas, she changed her business model and moved it online. Now Cindy teaches people how to make their own blends at home. The income she earned in Malibu was only enough for two trips to the grocery store and a car payment. That same amount of income pays her rent in Mexico. Years earlier she wrote a book about relationships and built an online coaching practice using the principles in the book. She was able to continue that business in Mexico. From Cancun International Airport she can fly to meet clients in the US or anywhere else in the world.

Cindy says that instead of working all year to scrape together the money to go on a two-week vacation, she now lives in a vacation destination and travels to work. Because she did not change her billing rates and with the much lower cost of living, she only needs to work for two weeks to earn the income to pay for two to three months of expenses. One day at lunch, Cindy overheard two men at a table next to her. One asked, "You want to know the Secret"? The other guy says "sure", and the first man tells him "Earn Dollars, Spend Pesos." Cindy knew exactly what he meant and knew that she had made the right choice.

What Becca and Cindy discovered is referred to as geoarbitrage, and it's a brilliant financial strategy. It simply means saving money by moving to a lower cost area while maintaining the same level of income. Not only can it reduce your living costs while increasing your quality of life, it is a very smart long term financial strategy. Housing costs eat up the lion's share of income for most middle class earners. If you can reduce your housing expenses by 50% or more that has a profound economic impact. You are able to reallocate housing expenses to savings and investments which means ultimately reducing the time it takes to reach economic satisfaction. I'll explain what this means and why it is important in Chapter 9.

In fact, my friend Diane reduced her monthly overhead by much more than 50% when she moved from San Antonio, Texas to Mexico. While she resigned from her university teaching post, she still charges the same fees for her career consulting and coaching services. Fluent in Spanish, she's picked up other teaching opportunities in Mexico. She's also launched a new business to teach others the tremendous financial benefits of living overseas. Below is a line by line comparison of Diane's current expenses in Mexico and her previous monthly expenses in Texas.

Expense Item	Mexico	US	Savings
HOUSING			
Rent	$650	$1500	
Electric	$100	$400	
Water	$0	$110	
Cable/internet	$75	$260	
Cleaning	$20	$400	
Cleaning Supplies	$10	$25	
Gardening/yardcare	$10	$100	
Mailbox services	$40	$0	
Misc	$20	$55	
TOTAL HOUSING	**$925**	**$2850**	**$1950**
TRANSPORTATION EXPENSES			
Car Insurance	$25	$110	
Gas and maintenance	$50	$210	
Tag/title	$5	$10	
Ferry tickets	$10	$0	
TOTAL TRANSPORTATION	**$90**	**$330**	**$240**
GROCERIES AND MEALS			
Groceries	$200	$400	
Meals & beverages out	$300	$600	
TOTAL MEALS	**$500**	**$1000**	**$500**

PERSONAL CARE

Massage 2 hr 2x month	$100	$200	
Chiropractor 2 x month	$50	$130	
Doctors visit	$25	$40	
Manicure - silk nails	$12	$45	
Pedicure	$12	$40	
Haircut	$10	$50	
Pet grooming	$17	$50	
Newspaper and mags	$0	$30	
Entertainment	$30	$100	
Misc	$25	$100	
TOTAL PERSONAL CARE	**$281**	**$785**	**$504**
TOTAL EXPENSES	**$1821**	**$5015**	**$3194**

Perhaps no other financial strategy can reduce your expenses by 50% as effectively as moving abroad. Doing so means it is unnecessary to sacrifice a great quality life now to (hopefully) have a bright economic future some day. As you can see geoarbitrage can provide the opportunity to travel the world, live in beautiful places, dine out frequently, and enjoy personal services such as massages and cleaning maid for far less than an average US middle-class budget. As you can see Diane Huth's move abroad delivered on all of this and much more.

Housing isn't the only budget item with extreme savings potential. In 2017 we bought a Yamaha 115cc Motor Scooter to get around the island. We paid about $1,200. That same scooter would have cost us $3,600 in the US. Our used 2011 Nissan Rogue cost us $6,250, half of what it would have cost us in the US. Our annual auto insurance policy with full coverage for two drivers is less than $300. Soon after she arrived, Diane bought a small used Chevy for $1700. We've both had car repair bills that were astonishingly low. Routine service calls to make repairs on air conditioners, pool filters or for locksmiths do not break the bank. Prices for consumer and household appliances like washers, dryers, refrigerators, stoves, and dishwashers are all about 50% less than comparable models sold in the US.

Myth #2: Healthcare isn't as Good

You Don't Always Get What You Pay For

When we talk about moving overseas, many people ask about healthcare. The majority are asking for information about cost, coverage, and pre-existing conditions. The United States spends 18 percent of gross domestic product on health care consumption. On average, other developed nations spend about half of that amount. In 2020, the annual cost of health insurance for a family of 4 exceeded $20,000 per year. A Kaiser Family Foundation survey found insurance premiums have increased over 55% in the last 10 years.

Unfortunately, the healthcare system is broken and Americans do not get what they pay for. If this is news, perhaps you have not been paying attention. The truth is there are far better healthcare systems in the world, that cost much less and deliver far superior care than the United States.

It is really shocking when you think about how much people pay for health insurance in the United States, a cost that continues to increase dramatically. It is amazing how many times we hear stories about insurance companies refusing to pay medical bills when you submit them or patients believe something is covered, then get surprised by bills they did not expect.

Without getting political, I will say this: I don't think it really matters which political party is in power. Maybe the US health-care system will somehow get better during the next 5 or 10 years, but I don't believe the system will change soon, regardless of which party get elected. There are just too many entrenched interests in the US healthcare system that are focused on maximizing profits. It is a sickness system; it is not a wellness system. In many other countries, a lot more resources are invested in preventative care. If you prevent illness, the medical providers can't bill as much which reduces corporate profits. That is the reality of the US healthcare system, and why it has not been reformed.

I do have some authority to speak about this because my first husband is a physician and I was with him through college, medical school and residency. I witnessed the evolution of the system away from the old delivery model in the mid 1980's to how it operates today. Now there are all sorts of interlopers, middlemen, insurance companies focused on maximizing profits for their shareholders, syphoning off precious resources from the health care system. There's a shortage of doctors in many places, especially rural areas.

My stepson Patrick went back to school at age 30 to become a radiology technician. He worked at a level one trauma unit in Tucson, Arizona, which meant he was very good at what he did. Unfortunately, he left that profession because he told my husband: "Dad, I could take an x-ray from this angle and it would show them exactly what's wrong, which bone is broken. But the insurance company won't pay for the x-ray from that angle. They'll only pay for this angle or another that doesn't show the doctor what he or she needs to see."

He became disenchanted with his career because he could not do what was in the patient's best interest. The doctor couldn't do his best work for the patient because the insurance companies call the shots. This bloated bureaucracy has created an entire cottage industry that dictates the practice of medicine according to billing codes.

A Twist on Medical Tourism

On August 9, 2019 the New York Times published an article about an American surgeon and a patient who flew to Galenia Hospital in Cancun, just across the bay from us, to meet for knee replacement surgery. The orthopedic surgeon was from Milwaukee and the patient was from Mississippi. Galenia Hospital is a world class medical center, accredited by both the Joint Commission International (US Gold Standard) and the the Canada International Accreditation (ACI) program, called Qmentum International.

The patient's insurance coverage was through her husband's policy at work. That company was self-insured for employee healthcare coverage and found it was cheaper for the company to fly the patient and the doctor to Cancun, Mexico, to perform the surgery than it was to perform it in Wisconsin. The surgery was half the cost it would have been in the United States. The patient incurred no out-of-pocket copays or deductibles, all her travel costs were paid AND she received a check for $5,000 from the company. The surgeon spent less than twenty-four hours in Cancun, for which he received $2,700. A sum that was three times what he would have been paid from Medicare.

The total cost of the surgery would have been $30,000 in the United States. In Mexico, it was $12,000. The per-night cost of a hospital in the US would have been $2,000, in Mexico, it was $300. The exact same medical device they used for her knee replacement was $8,000 in the United States and $3,500 in Mexico. So even after all the incentive payments and travel expenses, the total cost was half of what the company would have paid had the surgery taken place in the United States.

A friend moved down to the island a couple of years ago and like many who make this lifestyle change, she lost a lot of weight. She was quite heavy, so her extreme weight loss meant she had a lot of loose skin. She had a tummy tuck, her arms, and her legs done in an extensive surgery. It cost about $2,500; in the United States you would have to add at least another zero.

After living in Mexico for a year, I decided I needed a new health insurance policy. The company I chose required current medical records within the past 24 months. I did not have medical records that recent. The last time I had seen a doctor was in Florida 25 months earlier. As an alternative, the insurance company required a physical to see if I had any pre-existing conditions. I went to see Dr. Greta, a British general practitioner on the island. Dr. Greta gave me a full physical and provided a letter for the insurance company. The bill was 600 pesos, or about thirty dollars.

Today I pay $110 dollars a month for a global insurance policy with $5 million of coverage and a $2,500 deductible that is cut in half if I use an in-network provider. This policy excludes coverage in the United States except for emergencies. It does include up to 30 days emergency coverage in the US. One reason my policy is so inexpensive is that the insurance company will not be paying the exorbitant prices billed for care in the US (at least beyond 30 days). I am totally ok with that because the United States ranks #37 in quality of healthcare while spending more per capita than any other country on the planet, according to the Peterson-KFF Health System Tracker. If I want top-shelf medical care, I will not seek it in the United States.

While Medicare Part A and Part B (often referred to as original Medicare) do not cover you while outside the United States you can get coverage through Part C Advantage Plans. These plans often have zero premiums and cover emergency and urgent care medical services. In order to qualify you must have Medicare Part A and Part B and an address in the US registered with Medicare. That address will determine your Service Area and it need not be the same address as what is on file with the IRS. It may be prudent to use an address close to loved ones so if you need to return to the US for medical care you have some local support.

My husband Tom has this exact coverage. Medicare is there as a safety net in case of emergencies. Since the quality of health care is so good and the cost is so low in Mexico, we pay cash for routine visits and care. His recent visit to an ophthalmologist for a complete eye exam and prescription cost $750 MXN pesos or about $38 USD. The only challenge we've had is incessant telephone calls from United Health Care wanting to send someone for a "house call". It is clear that they receive reimbursement from Medicare for this "free" service. No matter how many times we tell them not to call, they continue to do so.

If you are an American expat who is shopping for a Medicare Advantage Plan here is a wish list that can help you evaluate and compare coverages.

1. Your Doctors in the Service Area will accept the plan and your prescriptions are covered
2. Avoid any limits on worldwide emergency and urgent care coverage
3. Look for no copays on worldwide emergency and urgent care
4. A Zero Premium Policy
5. Service Area coverage for Part A (hospital), Part B (medical) and Part D (prescription) benefits
6. PPO preferable to HMO so there is no need to get referrals from Primary Care Physician
7. Established and reliable insurance carrier with a large network that pays claims on time

Get Ready for Time Travel

Can you ever remember a doctor making a house call? Decades ago it was not uncommon for doctors to accept barter for medical services. A country doctor would happily accept chickens or other goods in trade from a patient as payment in lieu of cash. Those days are long gone but in many places it is common to pay a small fee for quality medical services including house calls.

One of our guest's children was running by the pool. He was specifically told not to run around the pool. But he ran anyway, fell and hurt his head. His parents took him to the emergency room where he had four stitches. The bill was $50. I do not know what that would have cost in the United States, but I am certain it would have been well over $50.

Another recent guest from New York dislocated his shoulder while zip lining at the water park. He went to the local hospital where he was informed he had to pay cash for the medical services. The doctor took an X-ray of his shoulder, then popped the bone back into the shoulder socket. The guest felt no pain, as he was too worried about the potential cost of his medical bill. The doctor took a second X-ray to be sure the procedure was effective. Our guest was directed to the cashier, and he was absolutely terrified to see the bill. When he summoned the courage to look at it, to his relief the invoice was $780 Mexican pesos! So the total fee for his emergency hospital visit and treatment was less than $40 USD. How much would that have cost in the United States?

A lot of people are concerned about the cost of prescription drugs. Nearly all pharmaceutical drugs are much cheaper in Mexico than in the US. In Canada and most other developed nations the government establishes price controls for the drug companies. In the United States, there are many effective treatments, procedures and drugs that are banned by the FDA but are readily available in other countries.

Vet bills are also less expensive. When I was living in California, I paid six or seven thousand dollars on sick pets. Chico, our first mate cat, sailed with us from Southern California through the Panama Canal, up to Florida, then down to Mexico and has over 7,000 nautical miles under his collar. He needed emergency surgery for urinary tract blockage. The bill was 2,500 pesos, or about $125. My friends tell me they paid $2,500 for that same surgery in the U.S. Chico spent three days at the clinic with 24/7 care. Our vet, Dr. Delfino also made three house calls after Chico's surgery. The house calls were $250 pesos, or about $12.

Wellness as a Health Plan

What if instead of treating the symptoms of disease, we treated the cause? If we take personal responsibility for our choices and our health, invest in educating ourselves about self-care, and take the necessary steps, we may become and stay healthier. Doing so will help ensure that we live well, while we are living longer.

In the 1970s, Debbie Seale-Kubeana and her husband spent their honeymoon on Isla Mujeres. In 1999 they bought a piece of property with a dilapidated building on it. About four times a year they would come down from Austin, Texas for vacations and stay in their building. In 2012, Debbie was diagnosed with Parkinson's disease, but continued to work as a nurse for another year and a half before deciding to hang up the gloves and enjoy life. Lee, her husband, decided to retire from the post office at the same time. Lee's new job is to keep Debbie's life stress-free. Stress is a big trigger for tremors symptoms and reducing stress is the best medicine to manage Parkinson's symptoms for Debbie.

After 37 years of nursing, Debbie's focus is on taking care of herself. She takes her meds, exercises, takes salsa lessons, has boxing lessons three times a week, and takes Spanish lessons. Photography is what she enjoys most, but she also sews and knits. Debbie has a knitting group that meets on Monday nights. She learned to play bongo drums and the ukulele. In fact, she is in a band with Cindy Lu (Spend Dollars Earn Pesos).

She attributes her good health to having an amazing group of friends and a strong support system. Their social calendar is booked almost every day. They have a Thursday group that gets together for happy hour at one o'clock in the afternoon. They have developed some close relationships and that does a lot for her health. She will tell you that her attitude is "Hooray for Parkinson's Disease." If it were not for that diagnosis, she would not be living the life of her dreams. Debbie's focus is on her HEALTH, not her disease.

Myth #3 There isn't as much economic opportunity overseas.

At age 35, Keesha Parker thought her dream of living in paradise would take another 30 years. She desperately wanted out of Arkansas, so she got licensed as a therapist in Texas. In May of 2018, during a break between clients, she was on Facebook scrolling and someone mentioned a Facebook group for therapists that work a hundred percent online. She joined the group. She spent a few months following the group to learn more about how people worked online. She contacted her licensing boards and both Arkansas and Texas blessed her proposed arrangement, provided she kept her licenses up to date. She took a course on how to set up her online business.

She gradually transitioned her existing clients to online, and all new clients are set up online from the beginning. Little did she know how smart reinventing her practice would be.

With the COVID-19 pandemic, her online therapy practice has grown and thrived in ways she could never have imagined.

Keesha says some people think she is crazy for moving to Mexico, that it's so dangerous. Many other people want this lifestyle, but they are unsure, they don't know how, perhaps they feel like they don't deserve it or that they are not capable of doing it.

One day while sitting in her favorite beach chair, under her favorite tree, she was looking around at all the beauty. It occurred to her that she always tries to get people to "think outside the box." Many of her clients struggle with social norms, family relationships and fitting in, and she helps them understand that it's okay to not be like everyone else. One day, as she took in the sights, smells, and sounds of her island paradise, she thought about her message of thinking outside the box. She realized "I am living outside the box!" Keesha never takes her lifestyle for granted, ever. Every single day there's gratitude.

Entrepreneurship at a Young Age

Cliff and his wife Chris are fellow sailors we met at the marina where we lived for our first two years in Mexico. They lived in Guatemala for 8 years, some of that time as liveaboards and also living in a house they rented with a view of an active volcano. They traveled the world extensively with twin girls. Cliff and Chris let them know from an early age there was a point that, as parents, they would no longer be responsible for them. When they became 18 years old, the responsibility for their lives would be theirs alone. Cliff feels at odds with contemporary parenting in the US, he says parents seem to lose sight of their children needing to be taught that ultimately their life is their responsibility.

There are twice as many 18-34 year olds living with their parents in the US than there were 20 years ago. Many are in debt and unable to get a job in their career field. Perhaps if those adult children, had they had their "horizons broadened" as Cliff calls it, would they be in that situation? If they had been exposed to what his girls saw: how inexpensive it can be to live in places where you ultimately have more choices at your disposal.

Cliff observes that when you get outside the United States, it is quite common to see child labor. He does not mean sweatshop labor, rather the philosophy that everyone has an obligation to contribute to the family. It is common to see younger people in some cases, 5 or 6-year-old children are out and about selling things. A little girl may sell handmade items, and she goes out there in a park or wherever people congregate, and she goes from person to person selling scarves or little handicrafts she makes. That money goes to help support and contribute to the family. Contribution is instilled in those children from an early age, and it is admirable.

They are not afraid of someone telling them "no" when they ask someone if they want to buy Chiclets or a scarf, they don't care. They know that if they ask 300 people to buy what they are selling, they will sell all their scarves or other goods and they will take the money home and put it in the cookie jar. That is the way that they are raised and it is the epitome of entrepreneurship.

Cliff does a quick comparison to entrepreneurship in the US and in other countries. He says, "Let's pick something very simple. Let's imagine that I want to make tortillas and sell them.

And the reason I want to make tortillas and sell them is because I make the best tortilla that the world has ever tasted. It is the most fantastic tortilla, and they are all made by hand."

"Now let us go to Central America. First, everybody in Central America loves tortillas, so that is not a problem. What do I need to make tortillas? Well, they are handmade. I've got two hands. I can handle that. The next thing I need is corn dough. So I go get some corn and I soak it in a brine solution overnight. Then I take it to the local corn grinder, which is on every block. I give him my corn and hand him two pesos and they run it through their corn grinder. And what I get back is a bucket full of corn dough."

"Okay, now I got my corn dough. All right, now I take my comal, which is a big flat pan, so it almost looks like the bottom of a steel drum. And I make a little fire and I set my comal on the fire and I grab a handful of corn dough and I slap it together and I put those little babies on top of that comal and heat them up and the smell permeates the neighborhood. Pretty soon, I've got people coming, wanting to buy my tortillas. Now, what have I invested? I bought a little bit of corn and I paid the guy 2 cents to grind it into dough for me and I'm allowed to sell my tortillas."

"One of my first customers will be the local official that comes by because he sees nothing wrong with what I'm doing and he's hungry for my tortillas, right? He is not going to arrest me and throw me in prison for not having the proper licenses. So, between the children out there working to contribute from an early age and the real entrepreneurial-ism that, when I was growing up, they used to call it the Great American Free Enterprise System. That was what made America attractive. And you know what? I thoroughly believe that 150 years ago in the United States, you were allowed to do what you could do to make a living and create those businesses that helped America thrive, but unfortunately, you have to go to Central America these days if you really want to see it in action."

"Now in the United States, if I am going to make tortillas and sell them it is a different story. First I need to have a business location, then I need to have several business licenses and I need to have a certificate from the health department. I must have a business bank account. I need a tax ID number from the federal government for my business, et cetera. We do not need to continue because it just gets more complicated from there. Bottom line, how much must I invest to make a handmade tortilla I think the world will beat a path to my door to buy because I make the best tortillas in the whole world? I have just invested a huge sum and I haven't even made my first tortilla. That is entrepreneurship in the United States."

Going Global for American Free Enterprise

The internet, technology and globalization have forever changed our lives, work, and business in many ways we do not fully understand yet. Remote work has been around for some time, I have used a virtual assistant company based in India for many years. Firms have outsourced work for even longer, but it was the COVID-19 pandemic that really brought home the truth that the location from which we work is unimportant provided you have reliable internet access.

There has never been a better time to work and get paid well while living overseas. Many, like Becca, Cindy, Diane and

Keesha can continue doing the same work overseas that they did in the US. Others see the opportunity to do something completely different. That might include starting a new business that can be run from anywhere in the world. Or if a profit producing venture is not of interest there are other ways you can find purpose and meaning in your new overseas life. How? That is what we'll discuss next!

CHAPTER 6:

Are You Ready for an Overseas Life?

Embrace Incompetence to Expedite Your Success

If you have never lived abroad before, odds are there is much that "you don't know that you don't know". That is called "unconscious incompetence" and it's the first stage of the four stages of competency in the "conscious competence" learning model. In this stage the "student" is unaware of even the existence of a skill or why the skill is relevant to them. Therefore, they are likely to also be unaware that they are deficient in the skill. There may be denial of the usefulness or relevance of the skill. The first step in moving out of stage one is awareness. The student must acknowledge that the skill has value and the student is incompetent in terms of possessing it.

As a practicing attorney, I frequently encountered unconscious incompetence when working with small business owners.

I worked very hard to save my clients from themselves. Often my skills as a transactional business attorney were not valued as useful or relevant which resulted in costly mistakes. I would explain to potential clients that the fee for my services was very small when compared to the fee my business litigation attorney colleagues charge. An ounce of prevention is certainly worth more than a pound of cure. At times the stories were heart breaking, especially when close friends like Brian and Michelle got hurt, whose story you will hear in Chapter 9.

I remember answering the telephone just before Tom and I were about to leave for the airport to go on a vacation. It was Brian, a favorite client who called to announce that he had just bought a business and he asked me to prepare a purchase and sale agreement. I asked him a few key questions about the business he told me he had just purchased and quickly replied "No, you didn't". Brian was a successful business owner but had a tendency to shoot from the hip.

I explained that under California law, when you purchase a business that has inventory there is something called a Bulk Sale Notice requirement. I quickly pulled up the statutory requirements, which included publishing a legal notice in the local newspaper. I sent it off to Brian and told him to run the legal notice as required by law while I was on vacation. I would prepare the documents and help finalize the business sale when I returned from our trip.

Another time I helped him unwind a messy business deal. Brian had entered into a verbal business partnership with an industry colleague. The plan to join their businesses didn't work out. Ultimately the woman's business did not bring the value to Brian's company he hoped it would. They agreed she would merely work as a commissioned salesperson for Brian's company.

Since they never entered into a formal agreement beyond confidentiality, my task as a lawyer was to both memorialize and unwind their verbal agreement. I drafted a creatively titled "Joint Venture Dissolution Agreement". Shortly after it was signed by the two parties, the woman unexpectedly died in a plane crash. Brian had dodged a bullet and her heirs would not be knocking on his door looking for their share of his company. It saved him the hassle and expense of protracted business litigation.

While it was not possible for me to help the unconsciously incompetent since they did not see value in my services, I could be a hero for clients who were in the second stage of competency: consciously incompetent. In this stage you KNOW you lack a skill and understand that the skill does have value. We all know making mistakes in life is just part of the process. As an attorney, some of my BEST clients were those who had made past mistakes (sometimes very costly) and therefore truly valued my services. They had a keen understanding of how my skills as a lawyer could help because they had suffered consequences in connection with unconscious incompetence. Experience had taught them the value preventive legal services and to seek out professional assistance the next time.

When you move abroad there is so much to learn. It is easy to romanticize the experience before you go and run into a harsh reality after you arrive. It is preventable? There are many sound strategies and skills that can help you adapt to your new country as quickly and easily as possible. We would much prefer to learn from the mistakes of others than make our own. For example, Tom loves to read about disasters at sea for the same reason they showed videos of boats sinking when he was studying to get his captains license. By learning what did not work, Tom would know what to do instead. Personally, if I read those type of books I might never leave the dock! But I am grateful that he reads them.

In fact, when we were preparing for our trip from California to Florida we did everything possible to discover what we did not know but needed to learn. We joined an international sailing organization, attended seminars, enrolled in online classes, spoke with sailors who had taken long sailing trips. We were like sponges, even though we were already seasoned sailors. We knew sailing 26 miles to Catalina Island is totally different from embarking on a 5000 nautical mile journey. We knew there were skills to learn, equipment to acquire and perhaps most importantly needed to be in top physical condition. The last one was key as we both contracted Hepatitis A and it was not fun at all. We didn't know there was a vaccine, but even if we had known I don't know that we would have taken it because we didn't understand the risks.

Gaining information and particularly knowing about mistakes made by others just makes sense. I've gained wisdom that way in connection with both personal and business matters. Using trial and error can work, but getting it right will cost more in time, money and energy. One of the richest men in the world, Warren Buffet, has repeatedly said the one investment that ultimately supersede all others is the investment in yourself. Constantly learning and improving pays huge dividends. Associating with the right people who are further along the same path will move you in the right direction. You begin by uncovering what you don't know that you don't know.

Take the *Are You Ready for an Overseas Life?* Quiz

When I begin working with clients, they start with the Are You Ready For An Overseas Life? Relocation Readiness Quiz. This tool helps clients assess where they are at in critical areas of life. In most cases clients are strong in some areas but weaker or not focused at all in others. The quiz can be very revealing. I encourage you to take the quiz and see what you learn about yourself. The purpose of the quiz in part is to help you to "know what you don't know". That is the first step of awareness as you move out of the unconscious incompetence stage and into the second stage of conscious incompetence.

Using this scale, rate yourself for each of the statements below:

0-3 = I haven't even started this yet

4-6 = I have given this some attention

7-9 = I'm doing really well here!

10 = I have totally Mastered this!

I. Research and Planning	Score 1-10
1. I have a clear, written vision of what I am wanting and I know what my successful overseas life looks like.	
2. I have geographically identified where I'd like to relocate to overseas.	
3. I have a plan to do all of the things I've always wanted to do.	
4. I feel very confident in my knowledge level of my destination country's rules, laws and cultural expectations.	

II. Finances	
5. I have a solid, location independent source of income.	
6. I have a budget, a strategic plan and I take consistent, daily action toward achieving my financial goals.	
7. I have identified solutions for banking, credit cards, money transfers, etc. for my overseas life.	
8. I have a Plan B ready to go if things don't work out the way I want them to.	
III. Disposition	
9. I am flexible, agreeable and non-judgmental toward others and their ways of life.	
10. I am prepared physically, emotionally and mentally for my overseas relocation.	
11. I am calm and patient when things don't go as planned, and I don't give up easily.	
12. I am not afraid to ask for help when I need it.	
IV. Communication	
13. I'm already fluent in or eager to speak the language of my destination country.	
14. I know nonverbal communication (body language) speaks louder than words.	
15. I have a plan for managing my relationships with the loved ones I am leaving behind.	
16. I enjoy and am adept at meeting new people, as I approach all interactions with respect, consideration and tolerance.	
V. Heath and Wellbeing	
17. I have researched available health care and insurance offerings in my desired location and am satisfied with what is available to me.	

18. I have coping strategies in place to address any feelings of stress, doubt and/or culture shock that are bound to come up.	
19. I am fully aware of what I consume, knowing that food is medicine.	
20. My mindset and lifestyle fully support my physical, emotional and mental health and wellbeing.	
VI. Commitment Level	
21. I am 100% committed to overcoming the challenges of relocating overseas.	
22. What was your biggest take-away as a result of completing this assessment?	
23. What are the top three challenges you are facing right now, as you prepare to move overseas?	
Total Score	

Moving abroad is fun, exciting and a little scary. Just like the success of our 5000 mile sailing journey was dependent upon our planning and preparation, these factors are critical to the success of your overseas adventure. There will be storms and rough seas. You will be scared at times. How will you handle those inevitable difficult days? What strategies can you put in place now so you aren't scrambling for solutions in the midst of a crisis or stress? Sailors practice man overboard drills so they have the skills at the ready before they need them in a crisis.

One of the most effective strategies for managing stress both before you leave and after arrival is to make self-care a non-negotiable priority. Scheduling time to focus on your well being and putting it on the calendar is crucial because if it isn't on the calendar it typically doesn't get done. I'll talk more about how to do that in Chapter 10. We can get off track and that's ok. What is important is that we know how to determine when we are off track and how to get back on.

Having systems in place to help you are a great start. I remember when the pandemic started and our entire island shut down. We didn't know how long it would last. I could imagine one day blending into the next and the next and the next. I made the decision to create structure in what could have been a blur. I was able to "return" to a Zumba class when it went online instead of in person in Florida.

Instead of focusing on worry and circumstances out of my control I thought about what I could do. I painted a mural I'd envisioned on our pool patio wall. Our vacation villa was always booked with guests, all of a sudden I had the time I needed to complete this rather large art project. I also worked on my business plan, took online courses and a few short months later I was ready to launch my business. I had a purpose during a very stressful time and having that focus had a positive impact in my life on so many different levels.

In fact, having a sense of purpose is THE most important driver of well-being. It does not matter what that purpose is, it just matters that you have it. Research shows it can literally save your life. According to a study published in the *Journal of the American Medical Association,* of the 7000 participants over age 50, those without life purpose were twice as likely to die, then those who possessed a strong sense of life purpose! Do not underestimate the importance of having purpose when you move abroad. That factor alone may well determine success or failure as you attempt to live your overseas dream life.

From the outside looking in Tiffany Lanier seemed to have it all: an IT job at the world-renown Mayo Clinic, she owned her own home, had a nice car, and a beautiful son. On the inside, something was missing. There was a deep void in her soul. Fortunately for Tiffany, fate intervened. When her best friend said she wanted a destination wedding, Tiffany generously offered to plan it for her. She was thinking Fiji but the bride said it wasn't a budget friendly location. Another friend suggested a little island in Mexico. They found a local travel agent who booked the trip for 19 people. Tiffany did the rest of the wedding planning by crowdsourcing, before the internet even existed.

The trip would change her life, by opening up a new world of possibilities and opportunities. She realized she could be an American and live outside her country. The thought had never occurred to her and it blew her mind. She met many business owners who were Americans and they were her age.

A year later she returned to that same island paradise. It was the first time she ever traveled alone. Walking along the beach on a moonlit night, Tiffany said the thought came "you have to move here" there was no question it would become her new home. She went back to Minnesota and submitted her resignation letter, rented out her house, packed up her 8-year-old son and their dog Lucky and moved to the island.

Tiffany decided to start a wedding planning business on the island. She had no idea how to do it and admits that her first 10 weddings were disasters. But after each one she sat down and wrote pages and pages of notes to learn from her mistakes. She became her own florist for the first 7 years because there wasn't one on the island. At the end of the day, Tiffany is a problem solver and that turns out to be a good thing if you are a wedding planner. Problem solving was also the driver in forming the Sisters of Perpetual Disorder many years ago. Tiffany started it as a support group for single women living on the island but over the years it has grown and evolved into so much more than that.

I asked Tiffany if she had figured out what was missing, if she knew what caused that void in her soul. She explained that she didn't feel connected while living in Minnesota. She feels connected in Mexico because she is passionate about her work and that makes her happy. Her work fills up her soul, and so do the Sister's meetings. She is able to travel to amazing places due to the remote and seasonal nature of her wedding business It all gives her a sense of community, support and the space to be who she really is. She did not feel that way in Minnesota or when she travels to other parts of the country. She experiences reverse culture shock now when she returns.

On a spiritual level, Tiffany says watching the sunset or feeling the breeze on her face makes her feel closer to God. She explains she did not find wedding planning, it found her. Tiffany's company Sunhorse Weddings has been named one of the 25 Most Influential Wedding Planners in the world!

Discover Your Freedom Formula

Now I am going to share the exact same process one of my mentors taught me when I was in transition. I was burned out and knew I did not want to continue the work I had been doing but I had no idea what I wanted to do next. It has been said "If you love what you do, you never work a day in your life!" Completing this exercise will help you find your Zone of Genius to focus on performing the work that you love. The work can be paid or unpaid. The exercise may also prompt you to remember long forgotten hobbies, pastimes and recreational activities. Have fun with it, but do not overthink it. Just write down what pops into your mind.

Step One: Make a list of your Top 10 Skills (What I am really GOOD at) and Top 10 Passions as described below.

Write down a list of the top 10 things you are very skilled at doing. Here are some questions to stimulate ideas.

What could I teach every single day?
What questions do others ask me?
What career or life experience do I have?
What have I learned to overcome?
What can I talk about for hours?
What can I do quickly and easily?

Write down a list of the top 10 things you are passionate about. Here are some questions to stimulate ideas.

What really lights you up?
What breaks your heart?
What makes you lose track of time?
What would you do if money was not a concern?
What are your hobbies or interests?

Step Two: Discover Your Zone of Genius
DO NOT GO ON TO THIS STEP UNTIL YOU HAVE COMPLETED STEP ONE.

DON'T EVEN READ the instructions for Step Two if you did not complete Step One. This is important because you do not want your Step One answers to be influenced by the Step Two process. Once you have completed Step One, draw a line through one passion and one skill from each column. Continue this process of crossing off, until you have only 3 Passions and 3 Skills left in each column. Now RANK them 1, 2, 3 with 1 being the one you are MOST passionate about. Do the same for your top 3 skills, with #1 skill being your TOP Skill.

Step Three: Listen to Your Higher Self

Just because you are good at something does not mean that it is what you should do. If it does not bring you joy, if it does not really resonate with you, why do it? I was a really good contracts attorney, but sitting behind a desk for 8, 10 or 12 hours a day pumping out legal documents was miserable. Just because you are good at something does not mean you should do it, especially if it does not bring you joy.

The next step may require some patience unless the answer literally jumps out at you right away! Then you are very blessed indeed. Congratulations! If you are like most of us, the next step is letting this information simmer and letting the subconscious do the work. If you meditate, then do as my mentor suggested and ponder the results and see what comes up.

Your goal is to let your creative mind go to work and guide you in the direction that is best. If you feel stuck, ask those who know and care about you, some of the questions from Step One, particularly when it comes to skills.

Another way to get help is to ask for guidance in our Claim Your Dream Life Community. If you still aren't sure, that's perfectly ok, this can take some time.

Step Four: Celebrate Your Successes!

Grab a journal or notebook. Now make a list 100 life successes you have experienced. They can be small wins or big accomplishments you decide. Do not stop writing until you have reached 100 wins. Bravo! You have now created 100 examples of accomplishments you can refer to if/when you ever doubt about your abilities.

Your Freedom Formula may reveal itself at once as it did for one of our Dream Lifers. Susan was a successful business consultant who had been working with early-stage start-ups and businesses ready to go to the next level for years. But she was totally burned out and wanted to do something else but did not know what. When we met and first spoke, she was bubbling with new business ideas, some were very, very good. However, she recognized that some were long term projects and/or would require outside investors.

As we went through this Freedom Formula exercise, her answer literally jumped off the page for her. On both her Skills and Passions list appeared editing and copywriting. These are both very lucrative skills in high demand and are services that can be performed from anywhere. She decided to tell the business she was working with that she would not continue, once her contract finished. They had just hired a new executive director, so she thought the timing would be good for them too. Then an interesting thing happened. Susan told them of her new focus, and they asked for a proposal to provide them with editing and copywriting services!

So instead of having to sell services she had not provided to the marketplace before, she landed a ready-made "new" client. Her new focus allowed her to perform the work that she loved, and the business could supply her with that crucial first editing and copywriting reference. It was a revenue stream she could rely on while living anywhere, and still work to achieve her bigger, longer-term business goals. It was so wonderful to watch the process unfold in real-time with her.

Your passions and purpose can change and evolve over the years. Nash grew up in a family that owned restaurants. He has owned and sold restaurants in California and Hawaii. About ten years ago he sold his restaurant in Hawaii and took off on his sailboat to travel the world. He was ready for his next adventure with the funds to support it. He sailed from Hawaii through the Panama Canal and along the west coast of the Caribbean Sea. When he got to the Yucatan Channel, his transmission gave out. He called for help and was towed to a marina on Isla Mujeres, Mexico.

While waiting for repairs, he walked down Hidalgo Street, the pedestrian-only main drag filled with shops, bars, and restaurants. He noticed that it lacked a good sports bar. That was the end of his sailing adventure and the rest as they say, is history. Nash found a nice spot and opened what became the most popular sports bar on the entire island. It became so popular he outgrew the space. In November of 2019, Nash opened Snappers, the same name as his Hawaii restaurant. This venue is a huge sports and entertainment complex complete with a covered stage for live bands, two swimming pools, a huge boat-shaped bar, pool tables, and two air-conditioned dining rooms. He LOVES what he does and his new establishment.

Retirement just was not in the cards for Nash, there was something bigger for him. There are no accidents, his boat breaking down is what led him to his paradise. Sometimes we just need to get moving and our future will find us.

CHAPTER 7:

Your Fastest Path to Cash to Earning in Paradise

The idea of job security is DEAD! I get annoyed with politicians and the news media droning on about jobs, jobs, jobs. If you really want to look at job creation, look at entrepreneurship. We should be teaching, promoting, and supporting entrepreneurship and small businesses. They provide an opportunity to build wealth and design your own lifestyle. More than two decades ago, I started on the entrepreneurial path, and I have not had a 'job' in 20 years. At this point, I am unemployable by choice. Let's talk about entrepreneurship.

The Four Paths to Entrepreneurial Success

Before we discuss the Four Paths let's stop to consider what resources you already have. In the world of business, there are three basic resources: Time, Energy, and Money. Of these, most would agree that TIME is the most valuable. Energy can be replenished and there are always ways to make more money, but we never get more time. It is a finite resource. You always know how much money you have but you never know how much time you have.

When you work as an employee, you are told what to do with your time. When you own a business, you decide what to do with your time. Once a person realizes their most valuable resource is time, they tend to spend it on things that truly matter. As a business owner, you have greater control over your time and activities.

The world does not end when you miss your daughter's school award day, or your son's baseball game. However, the confidence instilled in your child when you make it a priority to be at award day or the baseball game and all those other special moments is priceless. Business ownership gives you the freedom to not only attend those games but to be the coach of the team if you choose! You can volunteer for school events, your community, your church, or other causes and enjoy those special moments without compromising your income.

Are you interested in going into business for yourself? If so, there are four basic paths to entrepreneurial success, each with multiple options. Understanding the pros and cons of each and how they differ will help you make a smart choice about which path is right for YOU.

There are four paths to consider: direct sales or network marketing, purchase a franchise, buy an existing business, or start your own business. All four paths can supply income and time freedom. The first three have the advantage of turnkey systems from the moment you begin your business.

1. Direct Sales/Network Marketing.

According to the World Federation of Direct Selling Associations, there are over 125 million direct sellers worldwide, doing about 180 billion USD in sales. That is some serious business! Most direct sales companies offer a proven business model, extensive free or low-cost business training and support, and have low overhead and start-up costs.

Direct selling is the sale of a product or service, person-to-person, away from a fixed retail location, marketed through independent sales representatives who are sometimes also called consultants, distributors, or other titles. Sales reps can create a team by recruiting other people and earn a commission for their efforts. Direct sellers are not employees of a company. They are independent contractors who market and sell the products or services of a company in return for a commission paid on those sales.

Although a slightly different model, I include affiliate marketing in this category. The major difference is that you typically promote a product, make a referral, and receive a commission. You cannot create a team by recruiting other people and earn a commission for their efforts. However, companies often blur the line between these two business models.

Great for First Time Entrepreneurs

This business model allows you to build a solopreneur business or, if you choose, create leverage by building a sales organization that can provide a passive income stream. Passive income means that if something happens to you and you cannot work, the money keeps flowing to you. If you have never been in business before, this is a very low-risk way to start a business. It is also a way for you to "test the waters" and see if business ownership is really for you while gaining valuable skills in the process. Since it is your business, you work at your own pace.

It is also a good choice if you just do not have time to start a business but understand the importance of having a "Plan B," and want to build a business on the side while still employed. Because start-up costs are low, it is a way to go for someone without access to capital. No experience, no problem, you earn while you learn the business. Direct sales can be a perfect way for those with time constraints to start a business. If you are currently a W2 employee, the fastest way to give yourself a raise is to start a direct sales/network marketing business on the side.

I transitioned from practicing law by affiliating with a direct sales company that offered legal services plans, a legal HMO if you will. At first, I offered plans to people I could not help as a business attorney. I eventually walked away from the stress, liability and accounts receivable that went along with my law practice and worked with the legal services company full time. Today, I still receive residual earnings for the work I did with that company well over a decade ago.

Low Start-Up and Overhead Costs

Startup expenses can be very costly with some business models. A major advantage with direct selling companies is low startup costs. Your overhead is extremely low because there are no employees, there are no insurance expenses, management hassles, or liability associated with having employees. Other expenses such as computers, software, Internet, cell phones, auto expenses, and home office expenses may be tax deductible. Be sure to ask your accountant or tax advisor for advice.

Direct selling combines the systems and proven success of a franchise model with the freedom of an independent contractor, without high overhead, large capital investment or employees. It is a business model that offers low risk, and high reward. Direct selling uses the most effective sales method known, word-of-mouth and referrals. Since direct selling rewards you based on results, there are no income guarantees.

Because the company has a vested, financial interest in your success you typically receive extensive individualized mentorship, training, and support. Combining training with consistent effort is the secret to earning money and succeeding in direct selling and in any other business. Direct sales business owners can also get paid for helping other independent contractors succeed.

Direct selling offers you a way to build relationships with other successful business owners who can help you build your networks and create more profit. And it's not all work. These companies also have great teamwork atmospheres, fun social events, and incentive trips to exotic locations.

"Direct selling teaches you basic critical life skills, real-life training you can use, not the theoretical business stuff you learn in school."

Robert Kiyosaki

All Walks of Life

According to the Direct Selling Association, in 2020, about 8 million Americans, from all walks of life, were involved in direct selling. I have had mostly positive experiences with direct sales companies. The first was not a financial success, but the skills training was invaluable. The second continues to supply me with residual income. The third was more successful than I could have ever imagined! If not for that experience, my husband and I would not be living the life we love today. Through it all, we have made many amazing lifelong friends. That is the key to success in the industry. Find a product or service YOU are personally passionate about and get going.

> "The beauty of direct selling is that it's all done for you, all you need to do is find a reputable company that offers a product or service you believe in and can get passionate about."
> **David Bock,** *The Automatic Millionaire*

2. Buy a Franchise

Franchising is the practice of using another company's business system. Advantages include immediate brand recognition, a proven business model, operating systems that deliver results, advertising campaigns, training, and other support services.

The upfront capital investment can be substantial and a return on investment can take several years. Franchise fees can run into the millions and that does not include employee salaries, local advertising, insurance, rent and utility costs or income for the owner while waiting for profits to be realized.

A franchisor typically grants an independent owner/operator the right to distribute its products, services, techniques, and trademarks for a percentage of gross monthly sales and a royalty fee. Franchise agreements can last from five to thirty years, and the contract terms often greatly favor the franchisor. Franchise agreements can be extremely complicated, so be sure to seek expert legal advice before entering into any agreement.

Turnkey Systems

The great thing about the franchise business model is that they supply turnkey systems for the business owner. In theory, the recipe for success is already proven and provided to you upon investing. You just add your time and energy. That is how it is supposed to work. But not all companies are created equal, so do your homework before joining forces with any company.

One potential drawback is that you must follow their systems. If you are a creative type or like to do things "your way," these business models are not right for you. You will need to search further to find the company that is the right fit for you.

What factors should I consider in choosing a company that is right for me? According to Harvard Business School, there are five factors you should consider to find the right company. They apply whether you want to become an investor in a company, a franchise owner, a direct sales business operator or even if you are just looking for a job.

1. Is the Company stable? How long have they been in business? What is their proven track record?

2. Is it a good product(s)? Is it something you would buy? How much competition is there for the product(s)?

3. Is there a need for the product in the marketplace? Is it something that people will buy?

4. What is the Compensation? How many product(s) do you or your company have to sell to make your desired amount of income?

5. The Timing. In real estate, it is about location, location, location. In business, it is about timing. Years ago, opening a cell phone store was a good idea, now they are everywhere.

In my opinion I suggest you add two more important questions to consider.

1. Is this product a good fit for you? Do you use it and love it yourself? It is so much easier to sell a product you are passionate about.

2. Is the company a good fit for you? Do you understand and agree with the company's mission? Are you comfortable working with the people in this company? Do you see yourself investing your time and energy to do everything needed to succeed with this company?

I believe it is extremely important to remember that it does not matter how strong a company is, or how good the product is, if you are not passionate about it you will not be happy or successful. It is up to you to do some soul searching and discover what type of business best matches up with your skills and experiences, aligns with your business and personal goals and about which you are the most passionate.

3. Buy an Existing Business

If you are a conservative future business owner, buying an existing business may be a good choice. If you go this route, make sure the business has a five-year track record. Engage your CPA and attorney to help you with due diligence and analyzing the business. Be sure the business is what it was presented to be before closing the deal.

A reputable and experienced business broker can be helpful in your search and in completing the transaction. Like real estate transactions, the seller usually pays the commission. Unless you are an expert in legal and financial matters, you will need an attorney and an accountant. If your current CPA and attorney are not experienced in business purchases, you might consider finding professionals who specialize in business sales as one of their primary practice areas. Always use an escrow company or lawyer that routinely handles business sales to settle the transaction.

Jim Silver was a successful real estate agent in the San Francisco Bay Area for over a decade before the 2008 real estate market collapse. He was done with real estate and ready to pursue his passion for underwater photography and scuba diving as a business. His preference was to buy a business rather than starting from scratch. He scoped out Belize but didn't find what he was looking for. He visited Isla Mujeres in 2008 and 2011 and made friends on the Island. In 2012 he was contacted about a dive business that had closed because the owner had died.

The dive business structure was already in place, Jim just had to revive it. There was a dive boat, which turned out to need more work than he thought (BOAT!) and a customer list. The most valuable asset was a great domain name. The sales price was right because Jim wasn't buying an operating business, it had already closed. He never thought twice about the business being successful. Jim reasoned that if he could make a living selling real estate he could make this business work. Thirty years earlier an unexpected leukemia diagnosis put his life in perspective. The dive business was the perfect Freedom Formula answer for Jim Silver.

What Type of Business Should I Buy?

Here are some guidelines:

Like Jim, select a business that makes you say, "I get to go to work today!" If you are eager to go to work, it will greatly increase your odds of success.

Choose a business that is within your area of experience, range of skills or natural tendency. No matter what type of business you choose, you will have competition.

The condition of the business, the sales price, and terms of purchase should be favorable and make sense to you. Many businesses on the market are only for experts and "turn-around specialists."

The sales price, terms, conditions, and expected cash flow must fit your needs and financial condition. Do not overpay.

Have you discussed this with your family, and do they agree? How well does it fit in with your family's desired lifestyle?

Where Do I Find Businesses For Sale?

Online searches.

Word of Mouth.

Business brokers.

Suppliers within a particular industry.

Accountants and who service an industry.

How Much Should I Pay For a Business?

There are some guidelines for pricing businesses, but exercise caution as they are not precise. They can fluctuate with time, by geographic area, economic conditions, community attributes, business popularity, supply and demand, and social changes.

Price is usually determined by profitability and the value of the assets. The greater the likelihood that the business will succeed, regardless of a change of ownership, the higher the price you can expect to pay for the business.

The profitability record of the business is most important, but it cannot be the sole determining factor. There are many other significant factors that affect the purchase price. If the current owner has little impact on the business, it may be worth more than what the financial records show. The type of business also affects the price. Service businesses are typically the least expensive, followed by retail, manufacturing, and distribution businesses.

A good rule of thumb for small businesses is to never pay more than three times the value of "net," which is the total financial benefit to the owner. Net includes perks, fringe benefits, salary, and profit. Some businesses are worth less than one year's net income.

Never buy a business for all cash if you can help it. Typically, the buyer will make a down payment of 30-50 percent and the seller carries a note for the balance. As a buyer, you want to keep the seller interested in the business' future financial success. You will have recourse if the seller defaults on the sales contract or was less than honest about the true condition of the business.

4. Start From Scratch

This may be the most difficult path to take but it can also supply the biggest payoff. Instead of being given turnkey business systems, you must create them. This means more work, failures, and frustrations. You must enjoy a challenge and be willing to ask for help in areas that may be unfamiliar or difficult for you. By default, as a business owner, you are a salesperson. If you do not like sales, you will have to find someone to help. Enlisting mentors and advisors that can give you solid business advice and help you decide where to invest your time is essential. The easiest way to start a business from scratch is by freelancing.

There has been a long time trend toward freelancing for many decades. Perhaps now more than ever it is seen as a legitimate long term career option. Once you start on this path, you start to see endless opportunities and possibilities. The unemployment problem is not likely to disappear anytime soon and will certainly become more and more challenging for older workers. In fact, over a decade ago I specifically developed a training program to help guide what I call "forced entrepreneurs".

These were people who had lost their jobs and were unable to find new employment. After a long period, they were at a point where they just had to do *something* to generate income. This demographic had no experience starting or operating a business, or even realized that freelancing *means* you have a business! It is a different mindset and calls for a different skillset. One major difference is understanding how being efficient differs from being effective. It is not enough to be efficient in business, you must be effective.

What is the difference? I could be super-efficient in the way I handle my email messages. I may have folders and subfolders for all my email, rules set up for how they are handled and be able to find anything I want quickly. The question is: Does being efficient in handling my email put any money in my pocket? NO!

A great example is salespeople. The high payoff activity for salespeople is being in front of customers or clients who have the need and ability to buy what they are selling. They need to be in front of prospects to make money. Other activities they engage in may be prospecting, researching companies, telephone calls to set appointments, and driving to appointments may all make them more efficient, but not more effective at closing sales. As an entrepreneur, it is critical to quickly determine your most effective high payoff income activities.

Entrepreneurship is a Path to Wealth: Information that changed my life.

After my divorce, I was a 33-year-old single female scared about my future. I felt I needed to switch from a 100% commission-based job to something that would give me "job security". Being a lawyer sounded like a good choice. In 1993, I began my law school career. I completed a 2½ year program, passed the bar exam, graduated, and landed a 'dream job'.

One day a friend from law school called me a few years later and said, "Dawn, I can't do this anymore." She was a family law practitioner and had gone through a divorce too. She did not want to practice law anymore. She said, "I found something you need to take a look at." It was a legal services company, like a legal HMO. As an attorney, people think we know everything about divorces, DUIs, bankruptcies and criminal law, all sorts of things and we do not. She offered a way for me to refer people to other attorneys who could help them and build an extra revenue stream for me.

After I affiliated with the legal services company I quickly began earning $500-$1000 a month by enrolling people I could not help myself. At first, I only enrolled people I did not know because I thought if it does not work, I do not want to sully my reputation. If they do not know me anyway, then what the heck. I would follow up with each of them and ask, "Did they call you back? Did they help you?" They all raved about the service which actually surprised me a bit.

The company was hosting a convention in Las Vegas. I only knew it was a network marketing company, but now I wanted to know more, so I went to Las Vegas. I was already impressed with the people and their genuine passion for equal justice under the law, which can be expensive, if not elusive. What turned out to be a little reconnaissance mission changed my life. I do not believe I would be where I am today but for that trip to Las Vegas. One of the reasons was their keynote speaker, Robert Kiyosaki.

What I heard rocked my world. I had never been exposed to the information he shared. He said the poor and middle class trade their time for money by either working at a job or owning a job. Because there are only so many hours one can work, your income will be limited by hours. That sounded like me. I was a sole practice attorney, and I owned my job. I learned the wealthy do not teach their children to become employees or self-employed. They teach them to become business owners or investors, which means using leverage to generate income. That is done by owning a business with systems and employees or as an investor. Your money works for you, you don't work for the money.

I realized I did not want to be on the trading time for the money side of his cashflow quadrant, I wanted to be on the right side of the quadrant. I sat there taking in this new mind-blowing information and I was mad. I said to myself, "Oh my gosh, I've invested all of my resources, my time, the money (student loan debt), and the incredible energy to become an attorney. I wanted that brass ring, that job with the secure paycheck and here I am with a huge burden on my shoulders, of stress, liability, and accounts receivable". I realized I just owned my own dang job and I did not even like it!

I did love my clients. I had some of the most wonderful clients and did interesting work. I also remember them not being able to pay me, because they were business owners too. They had accounts receivable and clients that were not paying them so they could not pay me. What was I to do? I would not sue them or turn them over to collections. It is not that they did not want to pay me; they could not pay me. All these things were going through my mind while I was sitting there in that big convention center hearing this information for the first time. Why didn't someone tell me this? I had made a terrible mistake!

Then I recognized that I already had a growing, time leveraged business. Up until then I had only marketed the product through word of mouth but ended up by default with a team of 80 people in my network marketing organization. I put forth very little effort to build the network but here I was with a team that did their own marketing and sales while I collected a commission. I wondered what would happen if I really tried to work at it? That was in April.

I decided that I would go all in with the business. I rolled up my sleeves and got to work. I went to the meetings, I set goals to replace my income with this business, I worked hard, I was focused. By the end of the year, I had closed my law practice and in the first year I replaced my law practice income. The business is an insurance model which means I sell it once and get residual income for work I did almost 20 years ago. I found that once you have had a taste of residual income, you will go through a brick wall to get it. Although I have not marketed the legal service for many years, I could start it up at any time because I am still a distributor. Perhaps more importantly I still own the product and can't imagine not having affordable access to lawyers

Why I Quit Practicing Law: Lifestyle Security is Better than Job Security

Time leverage is achieving the biggest result with the least amount of effort. It is a strategy for business success, and about simplifying and finding the quickest route to the result you want. Once I understood what time leverage was, how powerful it could be, and saw the difference it could make in achieving my goals, I used my time in a different way.

I moved away from a "trading time for money" model (job security) and focused on creating time leveraged multiple income sources to support what I call Lifestyle Security. It is not that I never trade time for money. It just is not my primary source of income.

Several years ago, my husband and I took six months off and sailed our 48' sailboat, the "Santorini," from Southern California to Florida. We realized our dream of living near the water with a dock out front for our sailboat. While there we had a unique opportunity to work with a start-up network marketing company in the anti-aging space. In six short years we earned over a million dollars on a part-time basis and my husband was able to retire from engineering.

It has been over 20 years since I have worked for someone else, and we love the freedom of living our ideal lifestyle. It did not happen overnight. We worked hard but it was so worth it! I am not sharing this information to impress you. I am saying it can happen for you too. Unfortunately, too many people are still focused on finding that elusive "job security". Do not be one of them.

You can create your own Lifestyle Security by designing and building a business that does not need you to run it. How? That is next!

Can You Solve a Problem?

Want to know the key to success in business: solve a problem. Simple? Yes, that is what people pay for. If you can find a problem that people want to solve and are willing to pay to solve it, you can create a successful business.

Who Do You Serve?

In business, you must decide exactly who your customers will be and learn everything about them. If you say everyone is a potential client or customer, then you will speak to no one and be ignored in the marketplace. Nearly all business gurus will tell you to select a target market or niche. Too many times, I have seen newbie entrepreneurs think their business can serve anyone and everyone. It may seem counterintuitive, but that is just not the case. The more focused and narrow your niche, the more clients you will attract.

Making a choice about who you will serve empowers you to create messaging that really speaks to those you want to work with, who have the problem you can solve. Think about the type of people you enjoy working with. Do their values align with your values?

Once you have identified the problem you can solve, the next step is figuring out who has that problem and how to find them. Ideally, they are already aware of their need to solve the problem, have the resources to invest in solving their problem and are willing to pay to solve it.

If your target market is overweight, middle-aged women, then find out why they want to lose weight? Do they want to wear a certain size of clothes or feel good about putting on a bathing suit or become healthier? Clearly identifying the why is more important than the way they get there. People buy with their emotions, not logic. Engage their emotions by showing them the results they want and explaining to them how your solution can help them achieve those results. If your messaging clearly speaks to them and they feel you know and care about them, they will self-select and essentially say "yes, that is exactly what I need right now."

What Holds Us Back

The reptilian brain is evolutionarily programmed to keep us safe. One of the roadblocks that hold us back is acceptance by others. We are worried about what other people may think of us. Why? It is based on fear of rejection by the tribe. What tribe? Many years ago, humans lived in tribes of 30-50 people. Our physical survival depended upon acceptance by our tribe. If rejected, our very survival was at stake. We could lose the shelter, food, and protection of the tribe.

Our lizard brain detects criticism by others as "danger." So, we choose conformity lest we be outcast. In our modern world, our physical survival may not be at risk, but we conform to peer pressure to keep from standing out, rising above, or playing a big game in our lives. We must give ourselves permission to ignore what others think, especially in matters about our own well-being.

Susan Boyle was mocked at singing contests and judged by her appearance rather than her ability to sing. Her mom encouraged her to audition for Britain's Got Talent. She was reluctant as Susan thought winners were selected for their appearance. To please her mom, at age 48, she summoned the courage to go to the audition. To her surprise, she won! Susan's first album I Dreamed a Dream, was UK's best-selling debut album of all time.

The Lesson: Our self-doubt and the doubts of others are only powerful if you make them be. There will always be naysayers and doubters. You must become your number one advocate and become part of a tribe that cares for and supports you.

Now that we have covered how to make money overseas, let's talk about the more important part: It's not how much you make, it's how much you keep. That is the name of the next chapter.

CHAPTER 8:

It's Not How Much You Make, It's How Much You Keep

By Far Your Biggest Expense

Globally, 30 to 50 percent of income is paid in taxes. This statistic is high because it includes all taxes paid not just income taxes. There are a lot of hidden taxes we do not even consider. When you fill up at the gas pump, there are taxes included in the pump price: federal, state, and road taxes. Every time you buy something, you pay sales tax. In most countries of the world there is a value added tax called VAT with rates that vary by country. VAT is like sales tax in that it is a consumption tax paid when you make a purchase. In Mexico, the VAT is 16%.

Tax Freedom Day is the day when the nation, as a whole, has earned enough money to pay its total tax bill for the year. The date can vary slightly from year to year. In the US Tax Freedom

Day occurs on April 16th and in Canada, that date is in mid-May. That means you have worked enough to pay your share of the country's tax burden. Everything earned after April 16th or mid-May is yours.

State taxes can be different in each state. Auto registration in Florida was a fraction of what we were paying in California, because their system assessed the tax based on the value of your vehicle. Gasoline was a fraction of the cost in Florida because of the lower tax rates at the pump.

What is our duty as citizens with respect to taxes? Let us see what the United State Supreme Court has to say about the issue:

> "As to the astuteness of taxpayers in ordering their affairs as to minimize taxes, we have said that 'The very meaning of a line in the law is that you intentionally may go as close as you can if you do not pass it.' This is so because nobody owes any public duty to pay more than the law demands. Taxes are enforced extractions, not voluntary contributions."
>
> **Felix Frankfurter, US Supreme Court Justice**

Facts and Circumstances Tax Strategies

You are taxed based on your facts and circumstances so if you want to change your tax, then change your facts and circumstances! We discovered we had unknowingly made an excellent change of circumstances by moving from California to Florida before moving overseas. Had we moved from California to Mexico directly, we would have remained tax citizens of California and thereby subject to that state's income taxes. Because we moved to Florida first, we changed our tax jurisdiction to Florida, which does not have a state income tax. There are other ways to accomplish this aside from physically moving to a new state.

Moving overseas you will find that global tax systems have common regulations and individual countries will have more specific regulations within that general framework. You will commonly be taxed where you own property, have employees, an office, or a physical building, and you may be taxed where you pay contractors. All taxes are based on the specific facts and circumstances, unique to your situation. There are many nuances and rules that can change constantly which is why it is important to have professional tax advisors, one for your country of origin and one for the country in which you reside.

Legal tax avoidance strategies lower your tax bill by structuring your transactions so that you reap the largest tax benefits using existing IRS guidance to pay only the taxes you are required to pay. To be clear: I am not talking about tax evasion, but rather a tax strategy called legal tax avoidance. There is a big difference! Here are some important concepts to keep in mind.

1. It is your money, not the government's.

While you must legally pay your fair share of taxes, it is possible to keep more money in your pocket. What could you do with those extra funds? You could donate a portion to your favorite charity, help family members pay for college, save for health care expenses, fund your retirement or travel. As the Supreme Court says: we do not owe a patriotic duty to pay as much in taxes as possible and in fact we are encouraged to pay only what is required of us. Would you prefer to choose where your money goes, or let the government to decide?

2. The United States government is insolvent.

There are two major economic problems: deficit spending and borrowing without limits. Together, I believe it is a lethal mix when it comes to the average taxpayer on several levels. Do a search for US National Debt Clock and you will literally see the meter running. With each passing second, the United States goes deeper and deeper in debt. At this moment, every man, woman and child in the US owes, on behalf of their country $85,504 per person

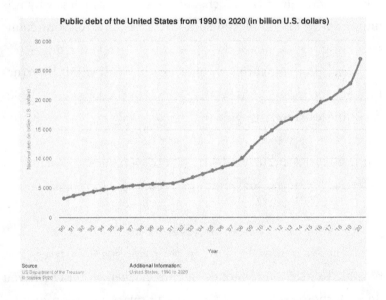

Public debt of the United States from 1990 to 2020 (in billion U.S. dollars)

Source
US Department of the Treasury
© Statista 2020

Additional Information:
United States, 1990 to 2020

Let us turn to the Federal Reserve System (Fed) it is not Federal, there are no Reserves and it is not a bank. It is a banking cartel, with immense power that has grown into a monster just as the Founding Fathers explicitly foresaw. They constitutionally forbid the creation of fiat currency, which is the creation of money that is not backed by a commodity such as gold. Thomas

Jefferson believed that allowing banks to create currency would only lead to financial ruin and said in his writings:

"A private central bank issuing the public currency is a greater menace to the liberties of the people than a standing army"

"We must not let our rulers load us with perpetual debt."

Federal Reserve History recounts "The Meeting at Jekyll Island": "In November 1910, six men...met at the Jekyll Island Club, off the coast of Georgia, to write a plan to reform the nation's banking system. The meeting and its purpose were closely guarded secrets, and participants did not admit that the meeting occurred until the 1930s. But the plan written on Jekyll Island laid a foundation for what would eventually be the Federal Reserve System."

There is no transparency as their meetings are not public. Fed meeting minutes are edited and not released until 30 days after the meeting date. Fed meeting transcripts are only released 5 years after the the meeting date. Anyone wanting information about the Fed's activities must file a Freedom of Information Act lawsuit and the Fed fights these requests regularly to avoid transparency. In over 100 years there has never been an audit of the Federal Reserve System. Despite not having a single elected official among its ranks, the Fed has morphed the U.S. financial system into a corrupt money laundering enterprise without congressional oversight.

Yet at present, the Fed is in complete control of the nation's monetary policy by governing the Federal Funds Rate (FED-

FUND). To accomplish this, the Fed buys and sells US Treasury securities using open market operations. If the Fed lowers interest rates, they buy more Treasury debt. When they do, the supply of investible debt is reduced. That causes the remaining debt to become more expensive, it lowers yield on those investments. Typically, short-term Treasury Bills are purchased or sold, which impacts the short-term FEDFUND interest rate and impacts the banking system's liquidity to achieve the desired result.

Quantitative Easing ("QE") is a fancy term for the practice of creating currency out of thin air, adding to the currency (money) supply, which debases the existing currency. The Fed takes the newly created dollars and uses them for large-scale asset purchases. By doing this the Fed manipulates not only the FEDFUND rate, but also interest rates across the board. QE transactions reduce supply, boost prices, and lowers yields in the overall markets.

In short, the Fed action encourages risky behavior and punishes risk-averse investors by artificially manipulating the markets. The free market doesn't exist. Instead, the Fed is picking winners and losers which has resulted in the largest wealth gap in over a century. The markets have become addicted to the Fed's free wheeling policies. Many experts believe the long effect of these policies will not be good.

In March 2020, for the first time in history, the Fed purchased corporate debt. This plan went much further than any prior QE, when the Fed only purchased government-backed securities. The Fed's stated purpose was to provide relief to companies during the global pandemic in order to continue to operate and pay their employees.

The unintended consequence translated to an enormous and unnecessary bailout of corporate lenders, underwriters and bondholders. Unfortunately, all that currency did not go where it was intended: creating and preserving jobs. The Fed required no assurances from large companies that benefited that funds they received would be used for that purpose.

Congress considered imposing such restrictions, but they did nothing to make sure funds went to companies with large work-forces or to prevent the proceeds from being used for executive compensation and bonuses, shareholder distributions and share buybacks. While the Fed's corporate debt purchase did little to benefit the US economy overall, the unintended consequences and huge cost to taxpayers merely decreased competition and reduced productivity.

What is likely to happen in the future? If you look at the historical supply of US currency, it was pretty stable going all the way up to 2008 until it spiked, it is how we got out of THAT financial crisis. I do mean currency, not money. Money is a store of value. Currency is merely paper backed solely by the full faith and credit of the United States (or that of the country doing the "printing").

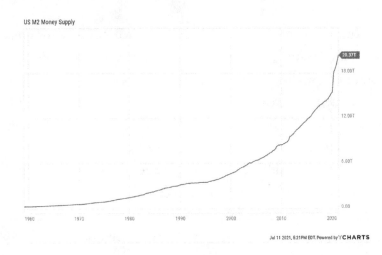

US M2 Money Supply

20.37T

18.00T

12.00T

6.00T

0.00

1960   1970   1980   1990   2000   2010   2020

Jul 11 2021, 5:21PM EDT. Powered by YCHARTS

Unfortunately, the US is not alone. Many governments have similar policies. Countries are printing currency out of thin air, when they do, every dollar (or other currency) you have becomes less and less valuable. The existing currency supply becomes diluted by the creation of more and more currency. If you study monetary history, you will see that currency debasement never ends well. It has happened many times before, although never at this scale. Many historians believe the Roman Empire fell because this is exactly what they did.

Take advantage of the incentives.

About 90 percent of tax codes concern tax deductions or incentives. It is why filing tax returns in the United States is so complicated. Governments use tax incentives to encourage certain types of activities, for example, agriculture, oil, solar, real estate, business startups, social change, and growth. To maximize the return on your investments, find out what the government wants you to do, and then get rewarded in the form of tax incentives by doing just that.

Think solar. There are all sorts of government incentives to create alternative energy sources. It might be a good business for you to start because of the tax incentives. Our friend in Southern California did just that and created a very successful solar business. His clients received state government rebate checks, and he received tax incentives to help grow his business.

If you are a W-2 employee, especially a high wage earner, there are smart legal tax strategies you can use to reduce your tax burden. My friend Laura sold her law firm and was bored so she got a job as a W-2 salesperson. Then she told me she paid eighty thousand dollars in taxes. Wow! Had she negotiated with the company to be a 1099 independent contractor operating her own business she would have been able to take advantage of business tax incentives, deductions and benefits available to her as a business owner.

Can you lower your taxes if you are a W-2 employee without quitting your job? Yes! Start a side gig. By starting a business, you may be able to allocate the portion of personal expenses, such as your phone bill, internet, or automobile, that you now incur to operate your business to business expenses. Be sure you understand and follow IRS guidelines and the advice of your accountant.

I invited my best friend to join me in the last direct sales company I worked with. She is a single woman with a good W-2 job, no kids, a low mortgage. Without a lot of tax deductions, she never got a tax refund check. In her first year in business with me, she got a tax refund for $8000. She was traveling and building her business at the same time. Travel expenses can be deducted as a business expense if you follow the rules and have properly documented them. My brother, David, is a single dad with four kids. The first year he joined me in the company, he got a tax write off to the tune of $4000. It really does pay to understand all the tax system incentives available to you.

For entrepreneurs and investors if you like to go to a certain place often then it makes good sense to invest there. You could buy an investment property where you like to vacation. Guess what? All those expenses are not necessarily vacation expenses. You may be able to prorate them and legally deduct a portion of your travel expenses as business expenses when you go there to tend to your investments. Remember, they must be properly documented and strictly follow the IRS guidelines to qualify as a deduction.

Will taxes go up or down?

Why does this matter? What I know is that over the years I have seen both tax cuts and tax increases. More often it was an increase, but I did not get focused on the changing tax rate. I kept my focus on tax incentives. Most believe we can expect tax rates to go up, particularly in higher tax jurisdictions.

Currently, states such as New York and California are experiencing a period of outward migration as people leave due to higher taxes. What do the states do to make up lost revenue? Raise taxes even more! Some Californians are paying an income tax rate of 13.3% and have decided to head to Nevada, Texas, or other states without income tax. Just by moving a few hundred miles away they keep more money in their pocket. Many New

Yorkers have moved down the coast to Florida where there is no state income tax.

For us, taxes were a major factor in our decision to leave California. I did quick math and realized by moving to Florida, not even factoring in income taxes, just taxes and fees for living in California, our savings would be more than $5000 a year.

We became Florida residents, lived there for six years, and then moved overseas. We pay taxes according to the last state we lived in before we left. Florida does not have a state income tax so we do not owe any taxes in Florida. It is something that you want to think about in terms of going forward. Policies can change rapidly and suddenly; a new law goes into effect, and it is too late. It is wise to consider these issues and have a good strategy. When a country gets in dire straits financially, history shows us they can do some strange things.

The Great American Tax Loophole

Ready to learn how to earn over $100,000 USD per year and pay zero taxes legally? This tax benefit is significant yet largely unknown. You may be aware that if you are a US citizen or a resident alien of the United States and you live abroad, you are taxed on your worldwide income. The US is the ONLY developed country in the world that taxes its citizens and legal residents on worldwide income.

However, you may qualify to exclude your foreign earnings from income up to an amount that is adjusted annually for inflation. For 2021 that amount was $108,700 or $217,400 per couple, if both partners qualify. To qualify for Foreign Earned Income Exclusion (FEIE), you must reside in a foreign country where you are permanently or indefinitely engaged to work as either an employee or a self-employed individual. Everyone must pass this test. Once you pass the first test, you must also pass one of two other tests to qualify: either the physical presence test or the bona fide residence test.

You pass the physical presence test if you are physically present in a foreign country (or countries) 330 full days during 12 consecutive months. The 330 qualifying days need not be consecutive. This test does not depend on the kind of residence you establish, your intentions about returning to the United States, or the nature and purpose of your stay abroad. You do not meet the physical presence test if illness, family problems, a vacation, or your employer's orders cause you to be present for less than the 330 days. The exercise is merely a matter of looking at a calendar and determining where you were physically located on each day.

To meet the bona fide residence test, you must establish a new home in a foreign country for an uninterrupted period that includes an entire tax year. The totality of the facts and circumstances will determine whether you have established a new home in a foreign country. Legal immigration status in the foreign country is required, a tourist visa won't cut it.

Once you satisfy the bona fide residence test, the 330 days of the physical presence test does not apply. You could legally stay in the US for several months and still meet the bona fide residence test. This is true if you have not moved back to the US and have not vacated your residence in the foreign country.

If you are a non-resident citizen of the United States (an American living abroad) you must still file tax returns and pay any US taxes owed. If you do not file a US tax return, you lose the FEIE tax benefits completely! Keep in mind this exclusion is for earned income. That includes salary, wages, or income and any money earned for performing services for clients done overseas. You file your normal tax return (e.g., Form 1040) plus Form 2555.

FEIE does not apply to social security or pension benefits, investments, or other types of passive income. If your primary source of income is passive income, for example, and if you trade stocks and options then you might relocate to Puerto Rico. If you live there, you will pay no tax on investment income. Neither the IRS nor the government of Puerto Rico taxes the passive income of Puerto Rican residents. Be sure to alert your tax accountant to this provision.

If FEIE applies in your situation, be sure your accountant or tax person is well versed in the applicable tax code. It could make a huge difference to your finances. In our case, when we moved to Southwest Florida, I went in search of a new accountant. I am pretty picky about who I trust to advise us on taxes and finances. I asked around the business community to see who the best people were in my new area. We have been very pleased with the firm's services.

After we completed the requirements to qualify for the Foreign Earned Income Exclusion (FEIE) I asked our accountant about it. He was not familiar with it because his clients are mostly Florida businesses and retirees. Many are snowbirds and they do not live overseas. Although he was unfamiliar with this provision of the tax code it does not mean he isn't a good accountant, it just means that his clientele was not the pool of people who took advantage of this provision. The truth is most people are not aware of this potentially huge tax benefit. It is doubtful your accountant, financial advisor or attorney will tell you about it because they are not aware of it themselves.

There is another good financial reason to move overseas full time. The reason is the tax loophole I just discussed. If you manage your own property, the revenue is not considered "passive." Remember the FEIE loophole only applies to earned income, not passive income. If someone else manages your rental property for you, then it is passive not earned income. You can still enjoy the other great tax deductions for income property you have in the US, just not the Foreign Earned Income Exclusion. Living abroad full time qualifies you for FEIE and allows you to take advantage of tax benefits of real estate investment.

Benefits of Foreign Investment

People are always asking us "Can you own property in Mexico?" The answer is yes! In 1973 Mexico passed the Mexican Foreign Investment Law which allowed non-citizens to buy property in Mexico with the exception of property located in the restricted zones (areas near national borders and the oceanic borders). In 1994 amendments to that law permitted non-citizens to buy property in the restricted zone indirectly through a 'fideicomiso', which is a trust agreement with a Mexican Bank. When purchasing land in Mexico be sure to buy it through proper legal channels. Rental property will have tax implications similar to the United States.

Due to a provision in NAFTA Mexico cannot confiscate any property other than for the public interest (like public eminent domain in the United States). The next chapter explains why investing in foreign real estate is such a great idea.

CHAPTER 9:

Foreign Real Estate Investment: An Offshore Dirt Bank

Don't Get Gringo'ed: Brian and Michelle's Story

About 20 years ago Tom and I were invited to attend a rather large party hosted by our dear friends Brian and Michelle. The invitation said they had a "surprise announcement." They had been together for several years and speculation was rampant, an engagement? An informal wedding? A baby? The party was buzzing with excitement when we arrived. It was a warm day and guests were socializing with cold beers and snacks, with heightened anticipation for the forthcoming news. Finally, the moment arrived, our hosts asked for our attention, which was eagerly and immediately given. I do not recall their exact words, but it wasn't what anyone expected.

They announced that Michelle had sold her adorable downtown Orange, CA Craftsman bungalow. They were moving to Mexico to start a surfing camp. They had invested in a beachside property with accommodations in Baja California on the Pacific Ocean, just north of Cabo San Lucas. They said they had Mexican "partners" who would assist with getting it started and help operate it. While we wanted to be as over the moon excited about it as they were, I was a bit more reserved and told Tom I hoped they knew what they were doing and had a good attorney. Things happened fast and before we knew it, they were off to Mexico.

It was about 6 or 8 months later that they contacted me. There were problems. The "partners" did not hold up their end of the deal. The agreement they made was not being honored. My heart sank. Even though I was a business transaction attorney, there was not much I could do for them, especially in Mexico. I referred them to our friend Doug, a fellow sailor, and Business Litigation attorney with experience in cross border cases. I wished them good luck for a happy resolution, but I had a bad feeling about it. Doug reached out to thank me for the referral and said he would do what he could to help them.

Over the next year, I would occasionally hear about the case. It was weak. They did not have a good contract. They did not use a local attorney to draft the contract or a Notario to ensure title to the property. (A Notario is a legal professional with a law degree, obligated by law to ensure the title deed is transferred and registered to the purchaser in the Registro Publico de la Propiedad.)

I do not know how much was invested, but it was substantial. Their legal expenses were not cheap. In the end, they got nothing and only threw good money after bad. They had been too trusting, too naive, they thought a verbal business agreement and some emails were sufficient. If you are ever in this position stop and ask yourself "would I do it this way in the United States? Absolutely not." So why would you do it in a foreign country?

The couple returned to Southern California with a shattered dream and depleted resources. They stayed for a while to replenish funds and then moved to Hawaii. Fortunately, they were young and talented, so such a mistake served as a lesson and not the devastating financial blow it might have been for others. They have a wonderful life now, so it ended well for them.

Over the years, I have heard many similar stories. It's called "unconscious incompetence" as I described in Chapter 6. I encountered it often as a practicing business attorney. This lack of awareness is the primary reason I created my real estate program 'How to Protect Your Wealth by Buying Foreign Real Estate'. My intention is that, for a low cost, potential investors can gain the knowledge they need to protect themselves and not get gringo'ed (ripped off). There are many traps for the unwary, especially if you don't know the rules or the legal process you need to follow to make sure you are protected.

Protect and Diversify Your Assets

What is FATCA?

In 2010 the United States Congress passed the Foreign Account Tax Compliance Act also known as FATCA. This law applies to every financial institution, located anywhere in the world, that does business with Americans. It is an overbearing and burdensome law that has caused many foreign financial institutions to flat out refuse to do business with Americans.

If they do, it means taking on a bureaucratic nightmare to comply with FATCA requirements. Essentially, through this law, the IRS has claimed jurisdiction over absolutely every financial institution on the planet that does business with US citizens. But there is a bit of good news: FATCA does not require owners of foreign property to report real estate owned in your own name. You can keep the information about such an investment private.

Real Estate vs. Other Investments

Other investments such as stocks, bonds, currencies, commodities and crypto may collapse, but housing and land will always be needed. By investing in foreign real estate, you own an asset that's not at the mercy of the wild roller coaster ride the real estate market has experienced over the past couple of decades in the US. Should there be another real estate crash in the United States, and many people do believe there's another bubble similar to what we saw in 2008, your foreign real estate is not subject to those same market extremes.

Our experience during the financial meltdown in 2008 was the main reason that my husband Tom and I bought property in Mexico. We were hurt badly in the real estate crash. We had three very nice properties go into foreclosure after their market values dropped suddenly and quite dramatically. We owed 1.1 million dollars on three homes suddenly worth $600,000 USD combined. It took quite a few years to dig out of that financial hole and we became somewhat jaded about investing in real estate again in the United States.

We rented for six years, got out of debt, and rebuilt our savings. When we were ready to invest in real estate again, we looked at properties on the west coast of Florida. We were shocked when we realized how inflated the values had become in a short period of time. It felt like we were seeing a similar phenomenon all over again, with rapid price appreciation in a rather soft economy.

We were determined not to be subject to those same market fluctuations again and potentially buying at the top of another real estate bubble. So, we started investigating other options and decided that it made the most sense to us to diversify our investments by purchasing real estate in Mexico. Oceanfront property is particularly expensive in the United States, as are taxes and insurance on those pricey properties.

Instead, we bought a piece of real property with multimillion-dollar views, investing a fraction of what it would have cost to buy something similar in the United States. Our property taxes are a little over $150 USD per year. We invested in a popular island tourist destination off the coast of Cancun. Since it is an international destination, the economy is diversified. We believe our foreign real estate investment is a much safer bet.

Wealth Preservation: Stop the Presses!

As I discussed in the last chapter, the Fed policies including "Quantitative Easing" can lead to inflation, which means your dollars do not buy as much as they used to. Investing in a foreign real estate 'dirt bank' is a way to protect yourself from sudden currency valuation drops and potentially any restrictive currency control rules that could be imposed if a financial meltdown were to occur.

When you think about the word "investment," what does that mean to you? Do you expect your investments to increase in value over time? That is not what we are talking about here. What we are talking about is preserving the wealth you already have. While these assets may appreciate in value over time, it's not the principal purpose. Holding them is not necessarily done for profit. This type of investment is made to make sure that if you have other investments in your home country that do significantly decline in value, you still have a portion of your wealth protected to fall back on.

When times are good, people are not as concerned with wealth preservation. But if there are clouds on the horizon, and a financial storm is brewing, that's when people become concerned. The primary question then becomes "How do I preserve my wealth?" Once the capital investments you have are at risk, wealth preservation plays a much larger role. The best time to prepare for a storm is BEFORE it comes!

Escape the Sue S. A.

As an attorney, I have seen the best of the US Legal System and the worst of it. While the Supreme Court Building Promises "Justice for All" and our Lady Justice wears a blindfold, you'll get the amount of justice you can afford. Many legal guardrails have been removed. Unfortunately, too many litigants and lawyers view lawsuits similar to winning the lottery. Damage awards are often too exorbitant compared to the actual harm sustained.

In the United States, anyone can sue you for any reason or no reason. If they do, you must defend yourself, which means finding and paying for a lawyer. If you do not, you will lose the case by default, and then the plaintiff can go after your assets with the judgement. It is one reason we still maintain the legal services plan we purchased in 2002.

I drafted a tight rental agreement that included premises liability for our Mexican vacation villa. The agreement states Mexican law governs the terms and the venue for bringing forth any legal claims is exclusively Mexico.

Just because our rental agreement explicitly states claims must be brought in Mexico and that Mexico (premises liability) law is controlling, does not mean a renter wouldn't find some US lawyer and try to sue us in the United States. If that were to occur, we have accrued substantial trial defense benefits over the years that will cover the cost of defense to blow such a claim right out of the water. It is a primary reason we still carry this coverage.

Investing in foreign real estate is one way you can legally keep some of your wealth overseas and out of reach of litigious plaintiffs. One key method of asset protection is holding assets outside the jurisdiction of your country of citizenship and residence. If all your assets are kept in your home country, they are fair game.

A judge or the government (state/local/federal agencies) can freeze your assets or confiscate them and take title to your properties. By holding foreign assets abroad, it becomes much more difficult for anyone to gain access to your property.

If you should ever be the victim of a frivolous lawsuit, and you own property in another country, a plaintiff will have to go to great difficulty and expense to navigate through a foreign court system and an international petition process to reach your assets. The very rich have always done this, but there is no reason you can't use the same asset protection strategies they do, to protect your assets.

Civil Asset Forfeiture

The Fourth Amendment to the United State Constitution is supposed to protect people from unreasonable searches and seizures by the government, however this protection has eroded tremendously over the past 35 years, with more encroachment of this fundamental right by the government and the courts.

In 1984, allegedly in an attempt to win the "War on Drugs" police agencies were given the legal authority to engage in civil asset forfeiture, meaning they can seize a portion or all of your private property with no due process whatsoever. To dispute such an action, you have the burden of proof to get it back. Reclaiming your assets after a seizure can take an exceedingly long time.

Federal, state, and local law enforcement agencies use civil asset forfeiture to take billions of dollars in cash and property from private citizens each year without convicting the owners of any crime. Instead, the government brings a civil action against the property itself, alleging that the property is "guilty" of being connected to criminal activity. This allows the government to take property without needing to charge the owner with a crime, prove their guilt, or otherwise afford them all the rights of a criminal defendant.

Often, the government gains ownership of such property automatically unless the owner files a claim for it within a short while. And when an innocent owner does file a claim, many jurisdictions put the burden of proof on the owner to prove their innocence, rather than requiring the government to prove their guilt.

By failing to protect property owners' constitutionally secured rights, civil forfeiture frequently leads to forfeitures of property belonging to innocent people. Often, the property owner is not even accused of being involved in a crime; it suffices that their property was used by someone else who is alleged to have committed a crime. Civil asset forfeiture is incompatible with due process, but the courts have failed to recognize that fact.

Private Right of Eminent Domain

Most governments in the world have retained the right of public eminent domain, meaning they can seize private property for public good. They typically must pay fair market value to the property owner when they chose to exercise that right. What is disturbing is this "taking" of private property for a public benefit has evolved away from the Fifth Amendment intent in a very disturbing way. The Fifth Amendment states, "nor shall private property be taken for public use without just compensation".

In 2005 the US Supreme Court in *Kelo v New London*, created a new government right to use eminent domain to take private property to give to developers to improve the local economy in a Connecticut town. In a very controversial 5-4 decision, the giant pharmaceutical company Pfizer was permitted to displace scores of senior citizens from a nine-acre tract so they could build a 750,000 square foot "urban village" business complex. Pfizer was to build a 26-acre Research Headquarters on an adjacent parcel. Nothing was ever constructed on the site where the homes were taken.

In the decade after *Kelo v New London* was decided, over one million homes in the United States have been taken using eminent domain for private benefit. The vast majority have been low income and minority property owners.

This story isn't an anomaly, a similar situation arose in Mount Pleasant, Wisconsin. In 2017, city officials were promised 13,000 jobs and $10 billion in private investment. Hundreds of residents were then forcibly removed from their homes for a hi-tech manufacturing hub called "Wisconn Valley." Few jobs ever materialized, the factory constructed was 20 times smaller than promised. The city was left on the hook for 40% of a billion dollars in loans, having built roads and infrastructure for the project.

Why does this matter here? One common objection about buying property in Mexico is "Well, the government can just take it." That statement turns out to be more true in the US than in Mexico, or other countries with the right of public (but not private) eminent domain.

The Dangerous Myth of American Exceptionalism

In 1990 only 4 percent of Americans held a US Passport. By 1997, it was 15%, then it jumped up to 27 percent in 2007. The biggest reason for the increase was the 9/11 tragedy when travel laws were changed and holding a passport became a requirement to go where they previously were not needed. By 2018, 42 percent of Americans had them, but that number still lags far behind other developed nations. For example, 66 percent of Canadians have one and 76% of United Kingdom citizens hold passports. Why does this matter? If you live in a bubble, you do not see what life is like in other places except as seen in TV or the movies. It is impossible to experience how others view your culture if you never leave.

American exceptionalism is a philosophy that the United States is intrinsically different from other countries because of the nation's history. America was founded on the principles of liberty, equality, individual responsibility, democracy and a laissez-faire economic system. This perspective views America as superior to all other nations, and therefore with the enlightened mission to help the world evolve in America's image.

I grew up with this worldview and had no reason to question it. To be sure, America has played an outsized role in the world and accomplished many great things. I never questioned this philosophy (nor was I aware of it) until I studied anthropology in college. I learned a word that fascinated me: ethnocentrism. I also realized that Americans are the worst offenders: the belief in the inherent superiority of one's own culture.

As I studied other cultures and societies, then backpacked across Europe one summer, I became keenly aware how damaging this philosophy can be. For the first time, I had an opportunity to see the United States through the eyes of people who were not Americans. Many Europeans I met loved the USA, and greatly respected her citizens. In France, I met people who remembered we helped end WWII and expressed their deep appreciation.

I grew up believing I was lucky to be born in the greatest country on earth! As I've traveled the world, I still believe there are many great aspects of America. There are also many, many great countries I've visited and where I would love to live. Unfortunately, America is no longer one of them. I'm thrilled to go back to visit, to be with our families and friends, to enjoy places like Minnesota in the summer. As time has passed, I sadly find that I hardly recognize my country.

On August 1, 2007, in my hometown, an eight-lane bridge over the Mississippi River in downtown Minneapolis collapsed on Interstate 35W. Cars, trucks and even a school bus in bumper-to-bumper rush hour traffic fell into the river below and its rocky shore. Thirteen people died, and another 145 people were injured, many of them very seriously.

The collapse of this bridge, an important freeway in a major city, prompted demands in Minnesota and across the country for immediate, substantial investment into repairing and replacing aging and unsafe infrastructure. Well over a decade later, while some improvements were made, tens of thousands of bridges across the country urgently needed to be fixed or replaced.

While Minnesota reconstructed the bridge in an astonishing 14 months, and put an aggressive plan in place to address structurally deficient bridges, the rest of the nation's infrastructure is in dreadful shape. According to Ray LaHood, a former US transportation secretary "America's infrastructure is like a third-world country." This situation is exceptional indeed, especially for what is supposedly the Greatest Country on Earth.

In February 2021, severe winter storms in the state of Texas resulted in a major power crisis. More than 5 million were left without power, some for several days and over 200 people died. Over 12 million Texans had water service disrupted due to pipes freezing and bursting. Similar crises occurred in Texas in 1989 and 2011, after which recommendations for upgrading Texas' electrical infrastructure to prevent similar occurrences in the future were ignored due to the cost. Lack of power and water are problems typically found in developing world nations, not the US.

In June 2021 a twelve story beachfront condo in Surfside, Florida collapsed in the middle of the night killing 98 people. Long-term degradation of reinforced concrete structural support in the underground parking garage, due to water penetration and corrosion of the reinforcing steel is the suspected reason. The problems were reported in 2018 but no structural repairs were ever undertaken. There are many, many 50 year old high rise condo complexes in Florida and other coastal areas. Structural engineering failures like this had been virtually unheard of in the US. Corruption during construction has been cited as a contributing cause of the collapse.

The Western United States has experienced extremely hot and dry conditions with deadly wildfires, electrical blackouts and extreme water shortages. Experts say it is the first human-caused "megadrout", which is defined as a severe drought occurring across a broad region for multiple decades. Sprawling cities fiercely compete with farmers and environmental interests, for this resource. To be sure, water scarcity affects every continent. According to the UN water use has been growing globally at more than twice the rate of population increase in the last century. Whether you stay in the US or move abroad access to water is definitely worth researching.

Taking clean water for granted in the US is no longer a reality across much of the country. According to the Environmental Defense Fund up to 10 million homes in the US still get access water through lead pipes even though they have been banned for over 30 years. There is no safe level of lead exposure.

While the decay I've described can be considered merely neglect, the decay of America's cherished values has been more willful. For hundreds of years, immigrants have been an important part of America's success and promise for the future. Immigrants have helped create a more vibrant economy and contributed to the nation's overall prosperity. One indicator is entrepreneurship, although immigrants comprised just under 14 percent of the total US population in 2017, they represented nearly 30 percent of the new entrepreneurs and were twice as likely as US born citizens to start a business.

Who are we as Americans? As a family? As Neighborhoods? As a State, our county and even as human beings? One of the United States' greatest strengths has been its diversity, which has come under attack in recent years. The global pandemic has seen the rise of another value, that of "American" individualism. Instead of the lofty goal of taking personal responsibility, liberty has morphed into an individual's private right and winning at any cost without regard to the common good. Community health and welfare has taken a backseat to self-interest and disregard for others. Is the idea that America is a Melting Pot, the people from around the world come and adopt the shared, lofty ideals upon which the country was founded, dead? Does the common good even matter anymore, or has American culture de-evolved into greed and self-interest as the new normal in both private and public life?

Let's turn to the subject of democracy in the United States. The events that unfolded in Washington D.C. at the dawn of 2021 have shattered the world's acceptance of American Exceptionalism. Many US immigrants fled politically unstable countries and never thought a political insurrection was possible in their adopted country. The peaceful transfer of power, respect for governmental institutions and an apolitical professional bureaucracy have traditionally kept America very stable.

Attend any Fourth of July celebration in the country, and you will see that Americans have had a quasi-religious belief in the Constitution and the power of our institutions to withstand any internal or external enemy. During recent years, it may be argued that this belief blinded many to very dangerous threats to our government that would test the resiliency of the Constitution. Democratic principles are not self-enforcing, the people must enforce and live up to them.

For two hundred and forty years America has been a shining example to the world of how the peaceful transition of power works in a democracy. The entire world was shocked on January 6, 2021 when the Capital was overtaken by an angry mob convinced an election was stolen. The President of the United States of America incited an insurrection. The Shining Beacon on the Hill sadly has lost its luster. I hope that it may not only be restored but there can be a more perfect union, and America may once again set a good example for the rest of the world.

Even if you decide not to leave the United States, it may still be prudent to have some of your assets leave the country. Having a Plan B is very wise, even if you never implement it. When we lived in Southern California, we had a Plan B in place if there was, say a 9.0 earthquake. We always kept the water tanks and the fuel tanks full on our sailboat the Santorini. A catastrophe of that size would surely mean no electricity: that means the ATMs would not work, nor would the gas pumps as they are all digital. It is likely freeways and other roads would be impassable due to collapsed bridges and overpasses.

Tom and I made an emergency plan to meet at the boat. He had a motorcycle; I had a bicycle. It might take a while, but I knew Katella Avenue, 2 blocks from my house was a straight shot to the Port of Los Angeles. Fortunately, that never happened and we never needed to implement our emergency plan. I am an eternal optimist; my glass is always full. That said, Tom and I firmly believe in expecting and hoping for the best, but also preparing for the worst.

I hope that America will shake off the problems and challenges I've described herein. She is a great nation that has been a beacon of light in the darkness. She can be once again. It is my intention that respect, compassion and love for each other and concern for the common good will return. We are social beings who need each other. If we don't care for our community and our planet, it will not end well. Yes, America is and has been exceptional, but that is also true of many other countries. We are not trees, and therefore are not required to grow where we were originally planted.

Only you have the power to decide whether it is in your best interest to stay or to go. Will you follow the herd or become your own authority? That's the topic of the next chapter.

---- **CHAPTER 10:** ----

Becoming Your Own Authority

Financial Stability & Economic Satisfaction

Perhaps you are familiar with the FIRE movement: Financial Independence-Retire Early. As you are aware by now I personally do not believe in the old concept of "Retirement", I think that it is an unworthy goal. Do you really want to "retire" at age 40? Nor do I believe "financial independence" is possible in an interconnected world with manipulated financial markets. None of us is an island and there are forces at play that affect our investments in ways we do not understand.

I have developed a preferred formula for financial stability and economic satisfaction. I call it the ESCAPE to Paradise Wealth Psychology Plan. It is an acronym for Economic Satisfaction + Community(& Cash!) + Abundance + Purpose + Estate Plan. I'll briefly explain the general principles for each below.

E is for Economic Satisfaction. I ask my clients to define their level of Economic Satisfaction. How much money is needed to support the lifestyle you desire? I do not believe there is some "magic number" to accumulate then sit back and never worry about money again. Why attempt to accumulate say a million dollars and attempt to survive off the interest when your assets earn zero percent or a nominal return? I prefer to focus on monthly cash flow and if a lifestyle upgrade is desired then go generate more monthly income. The focus is to ask "How much do you need each month to afford and enjoy the lifestyle that makes you happy?"

C is for Community. The pandemic has shown us the true importance of living in a place where people respect and care for one another. C also stands for a Cash strategy, holding physical cash, precious metals and other fiat currencies.

A is for Abundance of Assets, this goes way beyond financial assets and delves into all of the important intangible assets we possess and the legacy that we want to leave.

P stands for Purpose: When you are connected to your purpose everything changes. You are more committed, determined, courageous, willing to act and become fulfilled. It gives your life meaning and significance. Purpose attracts the right people and opportunities to you. It inspires you to do the things you would not otherwise do. It empowers you to create a legacy that lasts beyond your lifetime. Having a Purpose inspires you to be the absolute best version of yourself.

E is for Estate Plan. Your Estate Plan should address these four elements: Awareness, Access, Transferability and Financial Education.

We dive deeply into creating a customized ESCAPE to Paradise strategic plan in the Dream Life Academy training modules.

Foreign Residency and Second Passports

There are many reasons a second residency or passport is a good idea and an important part of any Plan B. Obtaining a second passport can provide you with a lifetime of broader choices of places where you travel, live, work, and invest. It is an investment that not only benefits you, but also helps future family members.

Many countries do not like US policies toward their country or globally. As a result, US citizens might be at risk if they visit those places. One of my podcast guests admitted that while traveling he would often tell people he was Canadian rather than American for that reason. So, freedom of movement and safety are two good reasons for having more options.

Under US Law (and other countries) dual citizenship is legal, so there is no requirement to relinquish your US passport. This myth is a concern I hear often when discussing this topic. In 1967 the US Supreme Court rule affirmed the right of dual citizenship in *Afroyin v. Rusk*, 387 US 253. Ever since, the presumption is that acquiring citizenship in another country does not signal an American's intent to relinquish US citizenship. However, the US requires all citizens to use a USA passport when entering the United States. Before 2015, it was a crime for US citizens to enter Cuba. That changed under the Obama Administration, and then those regulations were reversed leaving US citizens vulnerable to the whims of US government policy.

History is filled with examples of how a second passport can literally save your life. Many repressive governments have blocked their citizens from leaving. They can legally do it because your passport belongs to the government, not you, so they can seize it or suspend it at will. Having a second passport can provide security and peace of mind if political turmoil occurs or economic upheaval. Let's face it, most American ancestors left their home countries for a better life. It can also provide you with huge tax savings should you live overseas and qualify for the Foreign Earned Income Exclusion, as we discussed earlier.

There are two ways to obtain a second passport, and many more ways to obtain a second residency. The two paths to a second passport are by heritage or by economic investment. Citizenship by descent or ancestry is also known as citizenship by birthright. If you have parents, grandparents, or sometimes great-grandparents from a given country, you could qualify to become a citizen of that country. This method is very common in Europe with a huge upside: it means you could gain the right to live, work and invest in all 27 European Union countries. Some are very easy to obtain, others are not, but it is well worth investigating. If you don't qualify this way, there are still many countries where you can get citizenship after legal residency for a period of (usually 5) years.

The second method is citizenship by investment or economic citizenship. Citizenship is granted in exchange for financial investment in real estate, business or other foreign investment incentives. More countries have offered these programs in recent years, often due to indebted governments looking to raise cash and attract desirable immigrants. In the US, a path to citizenship is offered to those who invest $1.8 million in a business that provides employment for others. There are many options and not all require huge investments that only the uber-wealthy can afford.

If you give up your US passport and renounce your US citizenship you have expatriated. This option is also known as the ultimate estate plan. Since the United States taxes on worldwide income, it is the only way to get completely out from under that obligation. If you choose this path, be aware that you will incur an Exit Tax. Check with your tax advisor.

A US Department of the Treasury Report states a record 6,047 citizens expatriated during the first nine months of 2020, up from 2016 when 5,411 citizens expatriated.

Expatriates, or expats are individuals living and/or working in a country other than their country of citizenship. These are the millions of people who decide they want a brighter future and simply move overseas to live without a second passport. An interesting statistic is only about 1/3 of Americans have a valid United States Passport. It's nearly impossible to leave the country without one. So if you are looking for a good place to start, and don't yet have a passport from your own country then that's a good first step! After what we've just discussed, your instincts may tell you it is a good move. That's our next topic.

Attract what you want and repel what you don't

Remember the Beach Boys song "Good Vibrations" the song is about energy. Science has shown that we are pure energy. Have you ever noticed that when someone comes in the room they can "light up the room"? Conversely, you have probably experienced the opposite effect when "Debbie Downer" enters a room with negative vibrations and brings the energy level down. When you enter a room do you light it up or bring it down with your energy?

Like attracts like, so if your energy is positive and that is what you focus on, you will attract more of the same positive energy. The opposite is also true. We are magnetized energy and understanding this is important if you are focused on getting what you want. Everything we do causes ripples in the universe; quantum physics has proven this time and time again. We inhabit an energy field that literally unites our entire universe.

There have been many profound scientific discoveries over the past 100 years, making old textbooks obsolete and many findings that are not yet included in modern ones. Some of these "old truths" that are now false include:

- We are insignificant specs in a vast universe. (Darwin)
- There is nothing in the space between objects. (Newtonian Physics)
- Our internal thoughts, beliefs and feelings do not affect the world outside of us.

Interestingly, many concepts from ancient teachings, some thousands of years old, are now proving to be true by modern science. Ideas that used to be considered "woo-woo," are becoming not so woo-woo anymore. The big takeaway from this work is that we do have some control of what happens to us and that is very exciting! Knowing that, just how can we tap into this energy field and create what we want in our life? There is a recipe, we just need to follow it.

Trust Your Instincts

When Tom and I were sailing from California we were privileged to spend Christmas 2010 in Puerto Barillas, El Salvador with three other couples. Jim and Judy had spent the last six months there making repairs to their boat "Passion" after getting caught in a storm in the Pacific. They told us harrowing stories of the many bad things that had happened to them. Jim almost proudly proclaimed that he was "a s**t magnet." We all laughed.

They decided to leave the marina and continue south to Costa Rica with us. Their boat was about 35', our Santorini is 48'. That means our waterline gives us an advantage in speed. It was rather windy when we left, and they could not keep up. Jim flew the spinnaker sail to try and keep up with us. That type of sail is not meant to be flown in strong winds. Predictably, the sail shredded in a futile effort to stay with us.

After a harrowing journey, we made it to a protected anchorage at Bahia Santa Elena in Costa Rica where we had agreed to rendezvous. It was daybreak and we quickly fell asleep, exhausted after several sleepless nights in rough seas. When we went to bed, we were the only boat at anchor. When we woke up at about 10:30 am, we were delighted to be surrounded by all our friends from our last port. 'Passion' had come in and was at anchor off our stern, 'Mentor' was off our bow and 'Blue' was anchored alongside.

In comparing notes over cocktails, we all had a rough ride. The wind was still strong, but now all of us were safe in the completely enclosed bay. It was a calm oasis, a stunningly beautiful and completely empty bay in a conservation park area. Mentor's crew was on a mission as Cindy's dad was on his deathbed and she needed to catch a flight home. Although the Papagayo Winds were still howling a good 40 knots, Mentor left the next morning. They called Blue to report conditions as they rounded Key Point. Blue was trying to decide whether to leave that day or wait it out one more day. We listened to Mentor's report, "It's not bad, only blowing about 40 knots." We thought, Pacific Northwest sailors certainly have a different perception of windy conditions! Blue went and we stayed put that night. We were hoping the wind would die down so we could leave the next day. Jim and Judy were aboard Passion still anchored directly behind us.

We had lost our main anchor while trying to take shelter in a small bay along the coast of Nicaragua after a very rough and exhausting night at sea. A 50-knot puff of wind created too much pressure and the swivel parted, leaving our anchor buried in the sand separated from our anchor chain. We had a spare anchor, but it was not ideal for such a big boat in howling winds.

We took our inflatable ashore to explore and stretch our legs. We found a protected gravel beach that looked inviting. It was an abandoned fish camp, with a fire pit, old nets, shells, etc. We hung out and walked the shoreline for a bit. We were ready to leave and hopped back in the dink. As we got closer Tom said, "Is that an optical illusion, or is our boat REALLY CLOSE to Passion?" I dismissed it saying, "It must be an illusion."

As we approached Santorini, it was clear that our anchor had dragged, and our stern was now a mere 3 feet from Passion's bow. There we were, in this great big empty bay, with only one other boat and like a magnet, Santorini had dragged anchor to be dangerously close to Passion. How does that happen? We quickly climbed aboard, started the engine, pulled away and re-anchored. It was clear at this point we needed to get away from Jim and Judy. It was not personal, they seemed like a nice, albeit quirky couple. Their negativity was just too much, too close for comfort. We listened to our instincts and got far, far away from them.

In contrast, I remember meeting bestselling author Barbara De Angelis at a women's conference in California. I was a huge fan, having read several of her books and I credited her with helping me manifest my husband, Tom. When I went to shake her hand, she took my hand into both of hers and looked me straight in the eye and listened as I told her how much her work had affected my life. I distinctly remember feeling like we were the only the two people in the room. Barbara was 1000% focused on me and what I was saying. Her glow and positive energy were off the charts. I cannot recall having ever been near anyone with such a high positive vibration.

You are the Master Creator of Your Life

Are you controlling your thoughts or do your thoughts control you? Chaotic, disorganized thoughts lead us to indecision. Our mind is like a magnet, which draws to it, that which is similar to its thoughts. If your thoughts are negative, disempowering and focused on lack (what you do not have), your magnetized energy will draw those things to you. The more knowledge we gain, the better we will get at using energy constructively to bring what we desire into our lives.

Expectation is a necessary component needed to pull our desires toward us. Never expect what you do not want, and don't want what you don't expect to receive. One of the great truths is that we are creators, we can produce in the material world what we can imagine. Our creative energy is incredibly powerful, so we must learn how to use it properly. The most powerful mental state to enhance your creative power is Gratitude.

In my experience in leading large sales organizations, I learned there are two approaches people can take in business and in life. The difference in the results between these two 'mindsets' is nothing short of astounding.

In life, the vast majority of people live in a "reactive" state, they "wait for things to happen." They wake up and go through a mindless and repetitive morning routine. Then off to work they go, arriving, checking email, putting out fires. If there is a "to-do" list at all, typically the "squeaky wheel" gets priority. They are not in control; they are just reacting to what life throws at them. No wonder people feel anxious, stressed, and overwhelmed.

There are others who approach life in a "proactive" manner. When you adopt this mindset and implement a system of self-management you will change your life. The results you can achieve are profound. High achievers in multiple fields, disciplines and in Fortune 500 companies have this mindset. It creates balance in your life, so you can do more in less time. You set and achieve goals, even if you have never been good at it before. I attribute much of my success in life and business to changing my mindset and using a system of self-management.

Think about the difference between a thermometer and a thermostat. The thermometer merely measures the temperature. It is reactive and gives you what you want to know, the current temperature, and that is all. In contrast, a thermostat is proactive. It controls the temperature and dictates the conditions of an environment. If you are proactive, then you are controlling your environment and have the power to make it what you want it to be. You are in control of your actions, those actions can bring about your desired results.

Why wouldn't everyone operate on a proactive basis? Two reasons, one, they just do not know this is a better way and two, it takes effort to develop it as a habit. I am by nature a high achiever; I was good at making to-do lists (the really LONG ones) and at setting goals. Sometimes I achieved them, but more often I would fall short because I would set lofty and often unrealistic goals. Learning an effective system to achieve goals supercharged my performance. Achieving my goals became easier and more rewarding.

Implementing the Dream Life Achievement System can be challenging. No one really likes the process or uncertainly of change. Our primitive brain equates sameness with safety and security. Anytime we attempt change, even if it is to implement something we really want that will make our lives better, our instinctive resistance comes up. Expect to feel this resistance to change. It is normal and it is uncomfortable but it is part of the process.

Your Future is Found in Your Daily Routine

Planning is the foundation of being proactive. You give your mind the gift of freedom by thinking on paper and mapping out each day. It allows you to be creative and concentrate on more important matters. I used to pride myself on my ability to keep everything in my head which, as we get older, can be even more of a challenge to do that.

While learning a system of self-management is much more important than the type of *tool* you use, many studies show that the act of writing is much more powerful than typing. One study revealed that students who took paper notes learned more than those who typed them. Students who took notes by hand knew they could not get every word, so it forced them to focus on listening and digesting, then summarizing what they heard. If you use an electronic calendar, the system I describe will work for you, but I strongly encourage you to use paper and pen or pencil when planning.

Starting with a month at a glance calendar use a pencil to enter all your time specific appointments and events. This is your Master Calendar, so you do not want *everything* on it. This is for things like doctor appointments, conference calls, networking events, meetings, etc., events that cannot be changed around easily. You do want both business and personal time specific appointments on it.

Next, select a specific time each day, (e.g., the end of the business day) to plan the next day. Depending on your preference, you will use either a day at a glance (if you have a very busy schedule), or week at a glance. Then you will transfer the events that appear on your Master Calendar to the day you are planning.

Create a Future To-do List. When you plan the next day, you do not want to have more than 3-5 to-do items. By limiting the number of your to-dos each day, you will gain a sense of accomplishment and banish any feelings of overwhelm. Keep your Future to-do List within reach. As you go through the course of your day and more things "pop" into your mind you can quickly jot them down here. This practice helps keep your mind free of clutter and ends any stress around forgetting them.

As you plan each day, select 3-5 of your most important to-dos from your Future to-do List and put them in your daily calendar. If an item stays on your Future to-do list for too long, then perhaps it is not really a to-do? Quick five-minute tasks are not considered "to-do" items. Just do those as they occur.

Finally, reconcile your Master Calendar appointments with your selected 3-5 to-do items. Based on how busy with appointments your day is, select the ones that make sense given the time you have available that day. If you are easily distracted, use the time block method to complete your tasks. Estimate the time it will take you to do it, then schedule it in your daily calendar as if it were an appointment with another person. Be sure to include personal and self care activities such as exercise, meditation and family time.

One of the most important practices is scheduling appointments with yourself and your family. It is easy to make the excuse "I can't find time to…" fill in: exercise, reading, meditation, family time, etc. The fact is you will never "find" the time, instead the key is to "make" time. The way you make the time is to proactively schedule your day. You are the most important person in your life. Honoring your personal time will not only positively affect your health and well-being, but it also directly influences how quickly what you really want shows up in your life.

The Truth About Multitasking

You have undoubtedly heard the term "in the zone," it is frequently used by high performing athletes. It is a mental state of laser focus on a task, or sport. As you begin to operate proactively, remember how important it is for you to focus on the task before you, concentrating on only one thing at a time. A key component to making effective and long lasting change is focus.

Avoid distractions and wasted time by setting boundaries and fiercely protecting your time. Turn off any automatic notifications such as emails and other notifications on all your devices. YOU decide when you want to check and respond to them. Use email folders and files, only check them a couple of times a day.

I used to believe I was a great multitasker. Then I learned the facts about it. Humans are just not good at multitasking. Performance while multitasking has been shown to be worse than being under the influence of marijuana, and much like the effects of sleep deprivation. Although splitting your attention may feel like you are doing more, that just is not the case. Switching from task to task takes you twice as long to complete the work and produces twice as many errors! Instead of putting you "in the zone," multi-tasking disengages you from it.

Choose Your Team of Experts

No one cares about you, your assets, or your wealth as much as you do. You are ultimately responsible for your own life and wealth. How often have we read stories about people who got wiped out by a trusted advisor? Often it is because, before engaging that advisor, the person had not understood why they needed that advisor and exactly what that advisor would accomplish for them.

I make an effort to educate myself enough about a subject, to know how to determine if an 'advisor' is in fact an expert and can deliver on my expectations before I interview them. I used to network quite a bit when we lived in Florida and would often meet with financial planners looking for new clients. When they did ask for our business, I would ask them a simple qualifying question. Can you show me you are earning a six-figure income on a passive residual basis? If they could, I would agree to talk further. We look for financial advisors that are doing at least as well financially as we are.

I use a similar method when hiring business coaches and mentors. If they are not where I want to be, then how can they show me how to get there? I want to work with someone who has actually been there and done that. I always ask myself this question "Is this person a bit farther on the road I wish to travel?" when making decisions about who to trust. Then I always, always trust my gut.

Responsibility or Blame?

Have you ever had a big goal, worked hard toward achieving it and then have it completely ripped away? The dream and end goal are gone forever in a single moment? That happened to me when my first husband abruptly announced, "I don't want to be married anymore." We met in junior high school, dated during high school and lived together through college. He made the decision to go to medical school and become a doctor. He had my complete support as I worked several jobs, ran the household, and managed our finances. In March of each year, all US medical students are "matched" with teaching universities to continue their training in a residency program. Our match was with the University of California in Irvine.

Just a few short years later when my husband asked for a divorce, I was blind-sided and devastated. My husband was my future and without him I was lost. My world was shattered. I saw no path forward. My depression was so deep it nearly killed me. I had no support network. My friends and family lived 1,900 miles away in Minnesota. I was on my own to figure out what to do next, how I would go forward?

I remember a pivotal moment of decision in my life. After my divorce, I was so angry. I felt cheated out of our promising future and the endless possibilities. Having grown up in a poor family, I was very emotionally attached to a need for financial security. As I contemplated my future, I almost quite literally saw a fork in the road. My former mother-in-law was the motivation for my choice. I had a good relationship with her, but my husband did not.

To be fair, she could be difficult. My in-laws were divorced and they did not have a good relationship. The marriage had ended with a scandal that severely embarrassed my mother-in-law in a very public way. She never got over it. When we were together, she would often make very negative and hurtful comments about her ex-husband. She was bitter, and repeatedly played the role of victim. I recalled her behavior with sadness because it caused a huge rift with her children. They loved their father, despite his very public indiscretions.

At that pivotable point in my life, I firmly decided: I would NEVER play the role of victim. I had no idea what my future would hold, how I would fare financially, or if my broken heart would ever heal. I just knew at my core that I never wanted to end up a bitter divorcee. I would take responsibility for my part in the end of my marriage, and move forward. Years later as I studied personal development, I came to realize how important this moment of decision was for me.

Are you living your best life now? If not, what is holding you back? Earlier, we discussed the two methods of operating: Reactive or Proactive. Digging deeper, I believe that there are two distinct root philosophies that will determine whether we take charge and go for what we want in life. That philosophy choice determines whether we live a life of taking personal responsibility or a life of blame. One path leads to empowerment, the other leads to a life of disempowerment and playing a role of victim.

Paying Attention

Most people do not get what they want because they do not know what they want. Not knowing what we want can lead to feelings of uncertainty, fear and doubt. To avoid these unpleasant feelings, we find distractions and take a pass on the hard work of thinking. Instead of creating the future we want, we live vicariously through the experiences of others while time passes and the sand in our own hourglass constantly slips away.

The violence, destruction and negativity that 'entertain' us as we escape to movies, video games or social media only increases the emotions of fear, doubt, sadness, and anger. Our subconscious mind cannot distinguish between these fictional images and reality. As we discussed in Chapter 4, these thoughts send the brain into fight or flight mode which releases toxic chemicals. Then we wonder why we get what we do not want. Feeding our mind in positive ways will have longer lasting tangible benefits. Can your body be healthy on a steady diet of candy? Just as we feed our bodies healthy food, we must make a similar conscious effort to feed our mind healthy thoughts. It is important to monitor both the external input and internal dialog taking place in your head.

As an exercise, practice paying really close attention to how you communicate with yourself. Do you praise or criticize yourself? Are you encouraging or discouraging when you think about doing something new? We all have different saboteur voices, and they typically show up when we attempt making a significant change. These voices can be negative, judgmentally harsh or critical (the "Inner Critic").

This negative self-talk originates from our subconscious. It tries to control you by using fear, doubt and worry to maintain the status quo. With practice you can train your conscious mind to really "hear" them. If you understand what the voices are saying and why then they will lose their power over you. When we step out of our comfort zone and plan to implement big changes, these voices appear. These saboteurs have an important mission: to ensure you don't change. They often use the "images" from your past that were recorded by your subconscious.

Perhaps it's a well-meaning, but disempowering parent, teacher or counselor that said you weren't good at something. Your saboteur voices might show up as an authority figure who "makes the case" on why what you are contemplating is unwise, risky or dangerous. It is an internal battle for power that will ultimately determine "who" has control of your life and your dreams.

You can be sure they are present when these two dream stealing questions come up:

- Just who do you think you are, doing something like THAT?!?
- Why do you deserve XYZ when other people (better, smarter, etc.) don't have it?

CHAPTER 11

Our Journey Together

We are coming to the end of our journey together and I hope you have enjoyed it as much as I have. I am so excited for you and your new life possibilities! We are at such an interesting time in history. While there are many obstacles, there are many more opportunities. We may only see them if we change our viewpoint.

Your biggest obstacle can be a negative subconscious. It will try to keep you safe but in doing so will hold you back from doing what can truly make you happy. We must work to reprogram our mind. We have been told that we are "too old" to make major life changes. But that is simply not true. We are not too old to be brave, to take a chance, to feel young, alive, valued and loved.

I hope I have helped you overcome the idea that you must be rich to live overseas. Do a one-month "beta test" and you will find out very quickly that nothing could be further from the truth. I contend you must be rich to continue living in the United States!

There are several strategies and tactics you have learned here. I hope that the most important one you walk away with is the importance of Community. Humans are social creatures if they do not receive love and the human touch they die. I urge you to find your tribe, your community and join in. Be a valuable member of a community, for both the physical and mental health benefits. Nothing could be more important for your health and wellbeing.

Make sure that the Community you join encourages you to use your creative imagination to build the future you want. Not everyone you meet will be supportive of using your creativity to take your vision of the future and turn it into reality. Some just do not get it, and that is ok.

Remember Who You Are

Quantum physics has proved that the universe is comprised of rapidly vibrating energy that is never destroyed but merely changes form. Science has proved our physical bodies are 99% energy and light, with only 1% being solid. Human beings and our universe are like Holograms, we are truly 99% spiritual. It is easy to forget that we are living an illusion that is our modern day life.

Our soul actually knows this. When we become restless in middle life it is the soul's deep yearning to stop living the illusion and connect with who we really are. At our core we know that nonverbal communication is much more powerful than verbal. The conscious mind has the power to communicate with and "sell" the subconscious what it wants. As human beings we are like a bottle with a message floating aimlessly in the cosmic sea, waiting for someone or something to help us remember who we really are. I encourage you to open the bottle.

You have learned the importance of controlling your thoughts and have learned techniques to help you do just that. The first step is awareness. When you are attuned and aware you cannot help but hear those "voices" speaking to you. Practice Awareness, it is a valuable exercise whether or not you move overseas.

Use the Tools and Practice Them

Continue the Perfect Day narrative and if you are feeling bold, continue to refine a vivid 5 Year Vision Statement as the anchor that pulls you toward the future you want.

Creating your current and proposed budget is a powerful exercise that will demonstrate with your own finances that such a move not only makes sense but frees you in ways you can never imagine.

I highly encourage you to act Proactively in your life and commit to planning tomorrow before tomorrow comes. You will be astounded by how much more you can do when you cease living life on a reactive basis.

If you are looking to find your purpose or to create a new income stream, discovering your Freedom Formula can help tremendously. Investing time in this exercise will pay huge dividends. If you are not looking for more income, the exercise can serve as a compass. It can help you find more meaning in your life by focusing on what you are passionate about and the unique skills you bring to the table to help your new charity, cause, or passion project.

The universe has a funny way of leading us in certain directions. Like a bell that cannot be unrung, you cannot unknow what you have just learned. The decision is yours. Will you play it safe and stay where you are, or will you take that leap of faith and go for it?

I am driven to help people create lives that are as deeply meaningful as they are long, and to help them create a blueprint for the rest of their life. My vision is to create a community of people who never want to retire, but instead, want to live their best life for as long as possible.

I created the Overseas Life Redesign brand, and the Dream Life Academy to foster a community of like-minded people, peers who cultivate, harvest, and share wisdom with one another. If you are called to join us, we would love to have you join our Community.

I know that time is our most valuable asset, and we must consciously make the best choices for investing it so I would like to take this opportunity to thank you for spending your time with me in the pages of this book.

If you want to learn more, go to www.paradisechecklist.com and start dreaming again. We also invite you to join our Claim Your Dream Life Community on social media. I would absolutely LOVE to hear from you and about how the information I have shared in these pages has made an impact in your life. I look forward to connecting with you!

Dream Big and Act On it Daily,

Dawn

ABOUT THE AUTHOR

awn is originally from Minnesota. Early in life, she learned how systems make or break a business. She saw her dad's business fail, ending in bankruptcy. That experience fueled her passion for helping entrepreneurs. After a successful real estate career and a divorce, Dawn totally switched careers. She graduated Western State University College of Law with a Certificate in International Legal Process; and received the American Jurisprudence Award in Legal Research and Writing.

Dawn became a licensed California attorney in 1996, specializing in International Business Transactions. Dawn provided expert advice on intellectual property, mergers and acquisitions, distribution and franchising, and corporate law. As Managing Partner of Myers & Fleming LLP, she was instrumental in structuring engineering and construction projects for global industrial facilities worth over $2.5 billion dollars. Dawn co-authored, *Liability Limitation in Service and Consulting Contracts,* 44 Rocky Mt. Min. L. Inst. 22-1 (1998)

Realizing a legal career was not in alignment with her lifestyle goals, Dawn retired as a lawyer. She went on to become an award-winning Top Producer and popular Corporate Sales Trainer in the relationship marketing industry. For over two decades she trained and mentored thousands of entrepreneurs helping them launch, grow and maintain successful home based businesses.

In 2010, Dawn and her husband Tom left Southern California and sailed Santorini, a 48' center cockpit ketch, over 5000 miles though the Panama Canal and relocated to Florida, where they lived for six years. In June 2016, Dawn and Tom purchased Castillito del Caribe,(www.castillitocaribe.com) a stunning luxury oceanfront vacation rental villa in Isla Mujeres, Mexico. Seeking a beach lifestyle and a more vibrant culture, a year later they moved to the tropical island paradise.

Due to her courageous audacity to change careers, locations and lifestyles others took notice and asked for her guidance. Many Americans and Canadians she met are interested in purchasing foreign real estate so she decided to help educate them. Knowing first hand how mysterious the process can be and in order to provide transparency, Dawn created *How to Protect Your Wealth by Buying Foreign Real Estate* (www.offshoredirtbank.com)to help foreign buyers avoid pitfalls that await the unwary.

She launched a podcast in September 2019 to share success stories of other courageous souls who stepped out of their comfort zone to create a new life abroad. Overseas Life Redesign was born out of Dawn's burning desire to help others find community and support to live the life they imagine!

A free ebook edition is available with the purchase of this book.

To claim your free ebook edition:

1. Visit MorganJamesBOGO.com
2. Sign your name CLEARLY in the space
3. Complete the form and submit a photo of the entire copyright page
4. You or your friend can download the ebook to your preferred device

Morgan James
BOGO™

A **FREE** ebook edition is available for you or a friend with the purchase of this print book.

CLEARLY SIGN YOUR NAME ABOVE

Instructions to claim your free ebook edition:
1. Visit MorganJamesBOGO.com
2. Sign your name CLEARLY in the space above
3. Complete the form and submit a photo of this entire page
4. You or your friend can download the ebook to your preferred device

Print & Digital Together Forever.

Snap a photo

Free ebook

Read anywhere